MATLAB Graphical Programming

César Pérez López

Apress®

MATLAB Graphical Programming

ISBN-13 (pbk): 978-1-4842-0317-0

ISBN-13 (electronic): 978-1-4842-0316-3

Managing Director: Welmoed Spahr
Lead Editor: Jeffrey Pepper
Technical Reviewer: Dennis Kilgore
Editorial Board: Steve Anglin, Louise Corrigan, Jonathan Gennick, Robert Hutchinson, Michelle Lowman, James Markham, Matthew Moodie, Jeff Olson, Jeffrey Pepper, Douglas Pundick, Ben Renow-Clarke, Gwenan Spearing, Steve Weiss
Coordinating Editor: Mark Powers
Compositor: SPi Global
Indexer: SPi Global
Artist: SPi Global
Cover Designer: Anna Ishchenko

Distributed to the book trade worldwide by Springer Science+Business Media New York, 233 Spring Street, 6th Floor, New York, NY 10013. Phone 1-800-SPRINGER, fax (201) 348-4505, e-mail orders-ny@springer-sbm.com, or visit www.springeronline.com. Apress Media, LLC is a California LLC and the sole member (owner) is Springer Science + Business Media Finance Inc (SSBM Finance Inc). SSBM Finance Inc is a Delaware corporation.

For information on translations, please e-mail rights@apress.com, or visit www.apress.com.

Apress and friends of ED books may be purchased in bulk for academic, corporate, or promotional use. eBook versions and licenses are also available for most titles. For more information, reference our Special Bulk Sales–eBook Licensing web page at www.apress.com/bulk-sales.

Any source code or other supplementary material referenced by the author in this text is available to readers at www.apress.com/9781484203170. For detailed information about how to locate your book's source code, go to www.apress.com/source-code/.

Contents at a Glance

Contents

About the Author

César Pérez López is a Professor at the Department of Statistics and Operations Research at the University of Madrid. César is also a Mathematician and Economist at the National Statistics Institute (INE) in Madrid, a body which belongs to the Superior Systems and Information Technology Department of the Spanish Government. César also currently works at the Institute for Fiscal Studies in Madrid.

About the Technical Reviewer

Dennis Kilgore is the President and Founder DLL Solutions, Inc., a long-time OSIsoft partner, which delivers consulting and development services to customers in many industries including power generation, renewables, transmission, and distribution.

He has more than twenty-five years of experience in the design, integration, implementation, and maintenance of industrial process control and enterprise data historian systems.

As an avid developer, perennial conference goer, and self-professed geek - he enjoys occasionally giving presentations on recent projects and always looks forward to trading "tips from the trenches".

Since his introduction to MATLAB in 2010 during a visit to The MathWorks, Dennis has applied his passion for coding to the development of the "Direct Access™ Toolbox for Use with MATLAB", which simplifies data exchange between the OSIsoft PI System and MATLAB.

When not working, he can be found at home spending quality time with his family, whom he would like to thank for their unwavering support and never-ending patience with his workaholic nature.

Introduction

MATLAB is a platform for scientific computing that can work in almost all areas of the experimental sciences and engineering. This software allows you to work in the field of graphics, featuring some pretty extensive capabilities. The commands and functions that are implemented in MATLAB and other toolkits working with MATLAB are robust, accurate and very efficient.

MATLAB Graphical Programming is a reference for many MATLAB functions for working with two-dimensional and three-dimensional graphics, statistical graphs, curves and surfaces in explicit, implicit, parametric and polar coordinates. A wide array of short examples and exercises implement twisted curves, surfaces, meshes, contours, contours, volumes and graphical interpolation showing both the script and the result.

The book begins by treating two-dimensional graphics and statistical graphics. Then it delves into the graphic representations of curves in explicit coordinates, parametric curves and curves in polar coordinates. The next block of content is devoted to the log charts and bar charts, pies and histograms. Then we move into three-dimensional graphics, starting with warped curves, contours and surfaces charts, grids and contours. It then analyzes graphs of surfaces in explicit coordinates and parametric coordinates. It also devotes a portion of the content to display volumes, specialized graphics and special graphics commands in the MATLAB environment. Finally graphics for interpolation and polynomial fit are developed and special graphics commands are presented. If you are new to MATLAB or need a basic reference to MATLAB functions that are used in the book, then you may want to read the appendix to get up to speed fast. It can also be used as a reference to more general MATLAB functions for quick look up.

Also Available

- *MATLAB Programming for Numerical Analysis*, 978-1-4842-0296-8
- *MATLAB Differential Equations*, 978-1-4842-0311-8
- *MATLAB Control Systems Engineering*, 978-1-4842-0290-6
- *MATLAB Linear Algebra*, 978-1-4842-0323-1
- *MATLAB Differential and Integral Calculus*, 978-1-4842-0305-7
- *MATLAB Mathematical Analysis*, 978-1-4842-0350-7
- *MATLAB Numerical Calculations*, 978-1-4842-0347-7
- *MATLAB Symbolic Algebra and Calculus Tools*, 978-1-4842-0344-6

■ ■ ■

CHAPTER 1

MATLAB Introduction and the Working Environment

1.1 MATLAB Introduction

MATLAB is a platform for scientific calculation and high level programming through an interactive environment that allows for accurate resolution of complex calculation tasks more quickly than with traditional programming languages. It is the calculation platform of choice currently used in the sciences and engineering and in many technical business areas.

MATLAB is also a high-level technical computing interactive environment for algorithm development, data visualization, data analysis and numerical calculations. MATLAB is suitable for solving problems of technical calculation using optimized algorithms that for the end user are easy to use commands.

It is possible to use MATLAB in a wide range of applications including mathematical calculus, algebra, statistics, econometrics, quality control, time series, processing of signals and images, communications, design of control systems, test and measurement systems, modeling and financial analysis, computational biology, etc. The complementary toolsets called *toolboxes* (collections of MATLAB functions for special purposes, which are available separately) extend the environment of MATLAB allowing you to solve special problems in different areas of application.

It is possible to integrate MATLAB code in with other languages and applications, in addition to the distributed algorithms and applications that are developed using MATLAB. Taken together, the functions, commands and programming capabilities of the MATLAB ecosystem are a truly amazing collection.

Following are the important graphics related features of MATLAB:

- A high level technical calculation language

- A development environment for managing code, files, and data

- Interactive tools for exploration, design and iterative solutions

- Mathematical functions for linear algebra, statistics, Fourier, filtering, optimization, and numerical integration analysis

- Two-dimensional and three-dimensional graphics functions for visualizing data

- Tools to create custom graphical user interfaces

- Functions to integrate the algorithms based on MATLAB applications with external languages, such as C/C++, Fortran Java, Microsoft .Net, Excel and others.

The MATLAB development environment allows you to develop algorithms and analyze data, display data files and manage projects in an interactive mode featuring the Command Window, which is the hub of activity and is shown in Figure 1-1.

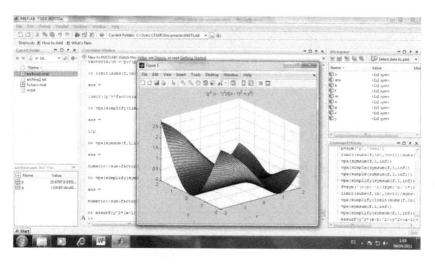

Figure 1-1.

1.1.1 Algorithms and Applications Development

MATLAB provides high-level programming language and development tools with which it is possible to develop and utilize algorithms and applications quickly.

The MATLAB language includes vector and matrix operations that are fundamental to solve scientific and engineering problems, streamlined for both development and execution.

With the MATLAB language, it is possible to program and develop algorithms faster than with traditional languages because it is not necessary to perform low level administrative tasks, such as specifying data types and allocating memory. In many cases, MATLAB eliminates the need of 'for' loops using a technique called vectorization. As a result, a line of MATLAB code usually replaces several lines of C or C++ code.

At the same time, MATLAB offers all the features of traditional programming languages, including arithmetic operators, control flow, data structures, data types, object-oriented programming and debugging.

An algorithm for modulation of communications that generates 1024 random bits, performs modulation, adds complex Gaussian noise and graphically represents the result is represented in Figure 1-2. All in just lines of code in MATLAB.

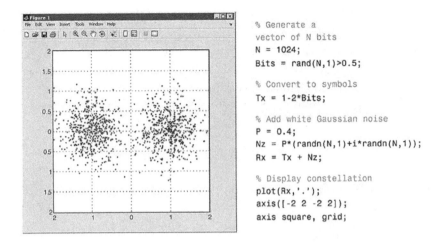

```
% Generate a
vector of N bits
N = 1024;
Bits = rand(N,1)>0.5;

% Convert to symbols
Tx = 1-2*Bits;

% Add white Gaussian noise
P = 0.4;
Nz = P*(randn(N,1)+i*randn(N,1));
Rx = Tx + Nz;

% Display constellation
plot(Rx,'.');
axis([-2 2 -2 2]);
axis square, grid;
```

Figure 1-2.

MATLAB enables you to execute commands or groups of commands one at a time, with no compile or link, to achieve the optimal solution.

To quickly execute complex vector and matrix calculations, MATLAB uses libraries optimized for the processor. For many of its calculations, MATLAB generates instructions into machine code using JIT (*Just-In-Time*) technology. Thanks to this technology, which is available for most platforms, execution speeds are much faster than with traditional programming languages.

MATLAB includes *development tools*, which help efficiently implement algorithms. The following are some of them:

- **MATLAB Editor** – With editing functions and standard debugging offerings such as setting breakpoints and step by step simulations

- **M-Lint Code Checker** – Analyzes the code and recommends changes to improve the performance and maintenance (Figure 1-3)

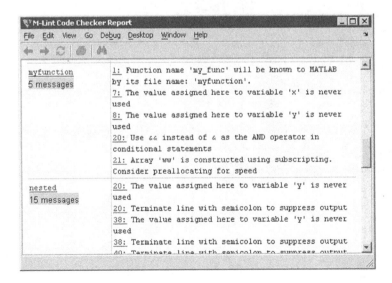

Figure 1-3.

- **MATLAB Profiler** – Records the time that it takes to execute each line of code

- **Directory Reports** – Scans all files in a directory and creates reports about the efficiency of the code, the differences between files, dependencies of the files and code coverage

You can also use the interactive tool GUIDE (*Graphical User Interface Development Environment*) to design and edit user interfaces. This tool allows you to include pick lists, drop-down menus, push buttons, radio buttons and sliders, as well as MATLAB diagrams and ActiveX controls. You can also create graphical user interfaces by means of programming using MATLAB functions. You can also expose figures or MATLAB algorithms on the web.

Figure 1-4 shows the analysis of wavelets in the tool user interface using GUIDE (above) and the interface (below) completed.

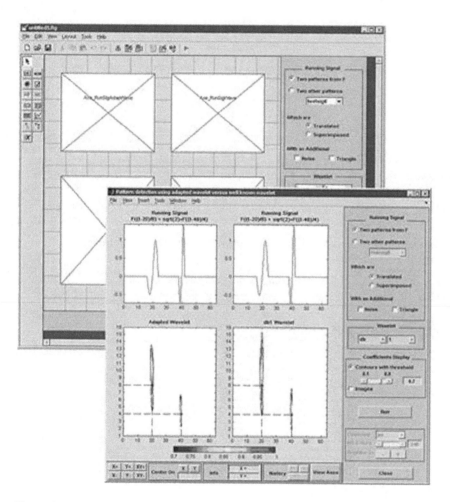

Figure 1-4.

1.1.2 Data Access and Analysis

MATLAB supports the entire process of data analysis, from the acquisition of data from external devices and databases, pre-processing, visualization and numerical analysis, up to the production of results in presentation quality.

MATLAB provides interactive tools and command line operations for data analysis, which include: sections of data, scaling and averaging, interpolation, thresholding and smoothing, correlation, analysis of Fourier and filtering, search for one-dimensional peaks and zeros, basic statistics and curve fitting, matrix analysis, etc.

Figure 1-5 shows a diagram that shows a curve adjusted to atmospheric pressure differences averaged between Easter Island and Darwin in Australia.

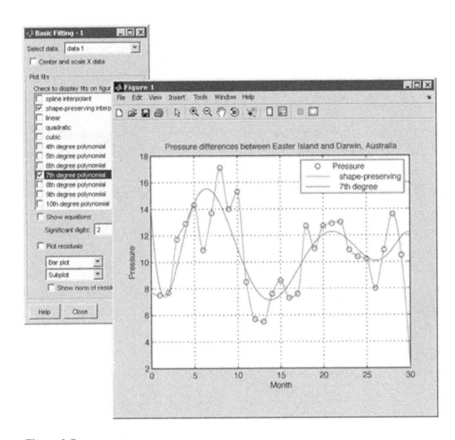

Figure 1-5.

In terms of access to data, MATLAB is an efficient platform for access to data files, other applications, databases and external devices. You can read data stored in most known formats, such as Microsoft Excel, ASCII text files or binary files of images, sound and video, and scientific archives such as HDF and HDF5 files. The binary files for low level I/O functions allow you to work with data files in any format. Additional features allow you to view web pages and XML data.

It is possible to call other applications and languages, such as C, C++, COM, DLLs, Java, Fortran, and Microsoft Excel objects and access FTP sites and web services. Using the Database Toolbox, you can access ODBC/JDBC databases.

1.1.3 Data Visualization

All graphics functions necessary to visualize scientific and engineering data are available in MATLAB. MATLAB includes features for representation of two-dimensional and three-dimensional diagrams, three-dimensional volume visualization, tools to create diagrams interactively and the possibility of exporting to the most popular graphic formats. It is possible to customize diagrams adding multi-axes, change the colors of the lines and markers, add annotations, LaTeX equations, legends and other plotting options.

Vectors functions represented by two-dimensional diagrams can be viewed to create:

- Diagrams of lines, area, bars and sectors

- Direction and velocity diagrams

- Histograms

- Polygons and surfaces

- Dispersion bubble diagrams

- Animations

Figure 1-6 shows linear plots of the results of several tests of emissions of a motor, with a curve fitted to the data.

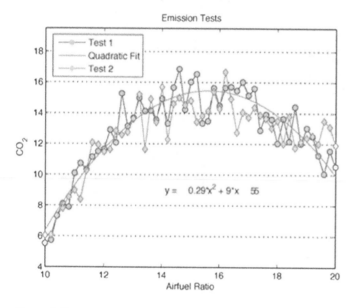

Figure 1-6.

MATLAB also provides functions for displaying two-dimensional arrays, three-dimensional scalar data and three-dimensional vector data. It is possible to use these functions to visualize and understand large amounts of multidimensional data that is usually complex. It is also possible to define the characteristics of the diagrams, such as the orientation angle of the camera, perspective, lighting effects, the location of the source of light and transparency. 3D diagramming features include:

- Surface, contour and mesh

- Diagrams of images

- Cone, pastel, flow and isosurface

Figure 1-7 shows a three-dimensional diagram of an isosurface that reveals the GEODESIC domed structure of a fullerene carbon-60 molecule.

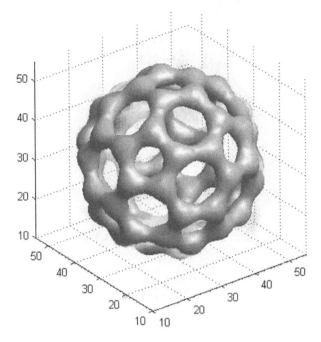

Figure 1-7.

MATLAB includes interactive tools for design and graphics editing. From a MATLAB diagram, you can perform any of the following tasks:

- Drag and drop new sets of data in a figure
- Change the properties of any object in the figure
- Change the zoom, rotation, add a panoramic view, or change the camera angle and lighting
- Add data labels and annotations
- Draw shapes
- Generate a code M file that represents a figure for reuse with different data

Figure 1-8 shows a collection of graphics, created interactively by dragging data sets onto the diagrams window, creating new subdiagrams, changing properties such as colors and fonts and adding annotations.

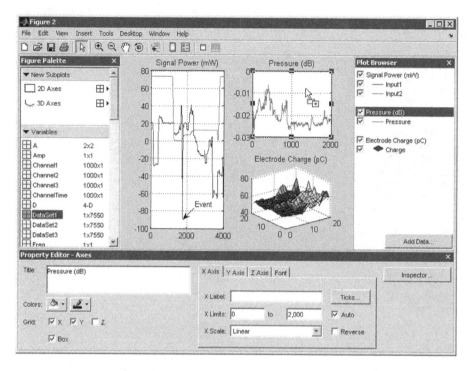

Figure 1-8.

MATLAB is compatible with the common file formats of data and best-known graphics formats, such as GIF, JPEG, BMP, EPS, TIFF, PNG, HDF, AVI, and PCX. As a result, it is possible to export MATLAB diagrams to other applications, such as Microsoft Word and Microsoft PowerPoint, or desktop publishing software. Before exporting, you can create and apply style templates that contain designs, fonts, the definition of the thickness of lines, etc., necessary to comply with the specifications for publication.

1.1.4 Numeric Calculation

MATLAB contains mathematical, statistical, and engineering functions that support most of the operations to be carried out in these fields. These functions, developed by math experts, are the foundation of the MATLAB language. To cite some examples, MATLAB implements the following math and analysis functions for data in the following fields:

- Manipulation of matrices and linear algebra

- Polynomials and interpolation

- Differential and integral calculus

- Fourier analysis and filters

- Statistics and data analysis

- Optimization and numerical integration

- Ordinary differential equations (ODEs)

- Differential equations in partial derivatives (PDEs)

- Sparse matrix operations

1.1.5 Results Publication and Applications Distribution

In addition, MATLAB contains a number of functions to document and share work. You can integrate your MATLAB code with other languages and applications, and distribute their algorithms and MATLAB applications as autonomous programs or software modules.

MATLAB allows you to export the results in the form of diagrams or complete reports. You can export diagrams to all graphics formats to then import them into other packages such as Microsoft Word or Microsoft PowerPoint. Using MATLAB Editor, you can automatically publish your MATLAB code in HTML format, Word, LaTeX, etc.. Figure 1-9 shows the M file (left) program published in HTML (right) using MATLAB Editor. The results, which are sent to the Command Window or diagrams, are captured and included in the document and the comments become titles and text in HTML.

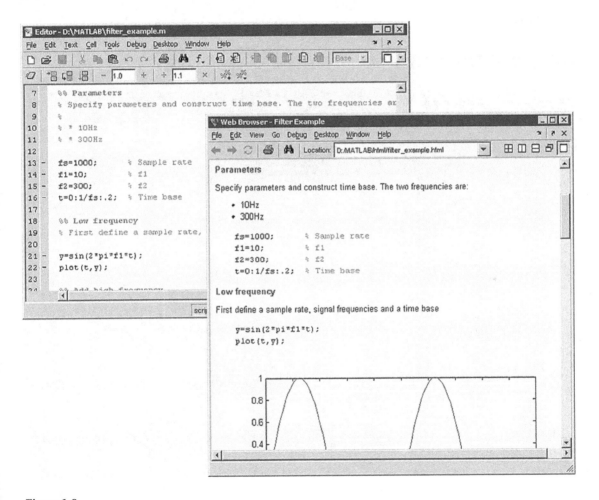

Figure 1-9.

It is possible to create more complex reports, such as mock executions and various tests of parameters, using MATLAB Report Generator (available separately).

In terms of the integration of the MATLAB code with other languages and applications, MATLAB provides functions to integrate code C and C++, Fortran code, COM objects, and Java code in your applications. You can call DLLs and Java classes and ActiveX controls. Using the MATLAB engine library, you can also call MATLAB from C, C++, or Fortran code.

For distribution of applications, you can create algorithms in MATLAB and distribute them to other users of MATLAB M file using the MATLAB Compiler (available separately). Algorithms can be distributed, either as standalone applications or as modules in software for users who do not have MATLAB. Additional products can be used to turn algorithms into a software module that can be called from COM or Microsoft Excel.

1.2 MATLAB Working Environment

Figure 1-10 shows the screen used for entering the program, which is the primary MATLAB work environment.

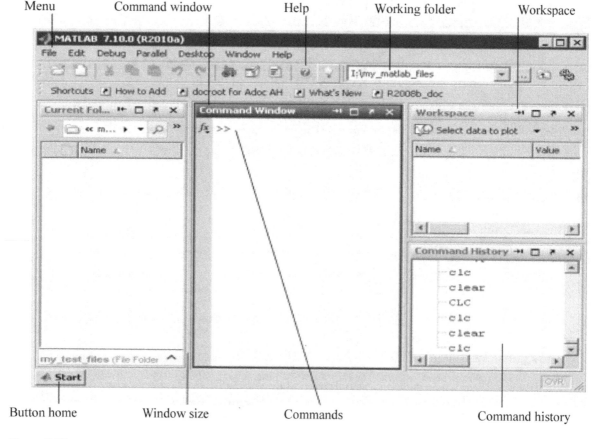

Figure 1-10.

The following table summarizes the components of the MATLAB environment.

Tool	Description
Command History	It allows you to see the commands entered during the session in the Command Window, as well as copy them and run them (lower right part of Figure 1-11)
Command Window	The window for interactive execution of commands in MATLAB (central part of Figure 1-11)
Workspace	Allows you to view the contents of the workspace (variables...) (upper right part of Figure 1-11)
Help	It offers help and demos on MATLAB
Start (Start) button	Lets you run tools and access documentation of MATLAB (Figure 1-12)

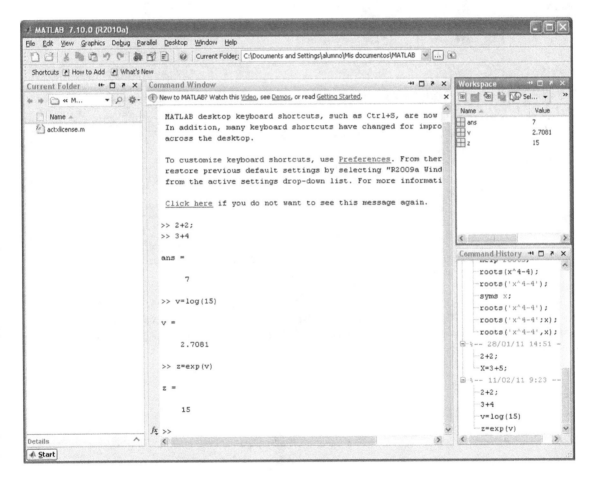

Figure 1-11.

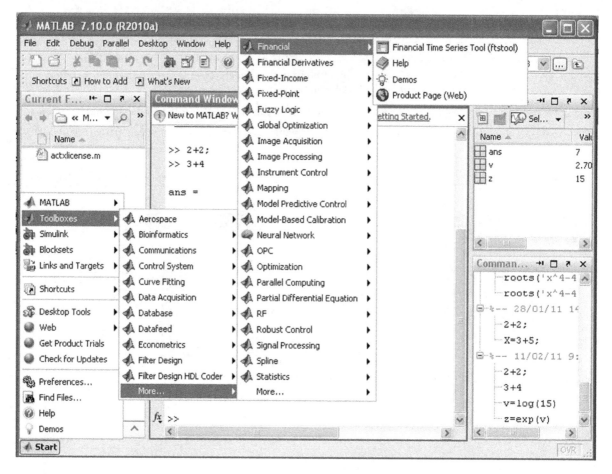

Figure 1-12.

Any input to run MATLAB is written to the right of the user *input* prompt ">>" which in turn, generates the response in the lines immediately below it. On completion, MATLAB displays the user input prompt again so that you can introduce more entries (Figure 1-13).

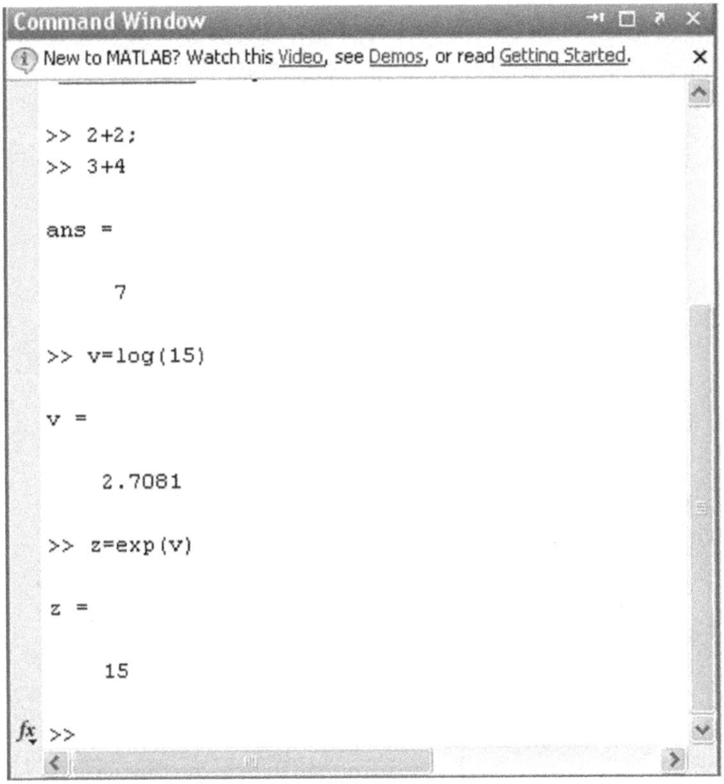

```
Command Window                              →| □ ↗ ✕
ⓘ New to MATLAB? Watch this Video, see Demos, or read Getting Started.   ✕

  >> 2+2;
  >> 3+4

  ans =

       7

  >> v=log(15)

  v =

       2.7081

  >> z=exp(v)

  z =

       15

fx >>
```

Figure 1-13.

When an input (user *input*) is proposed to MATLAB in the Command Window that does not cite a variable to collect the result, MATLAB returns the response using the expression ***ans=*** as shown at the beginning of Figure 1-13. If at the start of our input to MATLAB, we define a variable to contain the results, we can then use that variable as the argument for subsequent entries. That is the case with variable v in Figure 1-13, which is subsequently used as input in an exponential function call.

To run an input entry, simply press *Enter* once you have finished. If at any point in the input we put a semicolon, the program runs calculations to that point and keeps them in memory (*Workspace*), but it does not display the result on the screen (see the first input in Figure 1-13). After you have hit Enter, MATLAB will respond and when it is done, the *input* prompt again appears ">> " to indicate that you can enter a new command, function, etc.

Like the C programming language, MATLAB is sensitive to the difference between uppercase and lowercase letters; for example, *Sin (x)* is different from *sin (x)*. The names of all MATLAB built-in functions begin with lowercase. There should be no spaces in the names of functions or in symbols of more than one letter. In other cases, spaces are ignored. They can be used to make input more readable. To save time you can provide input for multiple entries separated by commas on the same line of a command,, and pressing Enter at the end of the last entry will run each of the MATLAB responses separately (Figure 1-14). If you use a semicolon at the end of one of the entries of the line, its corresponding output is not displayed.

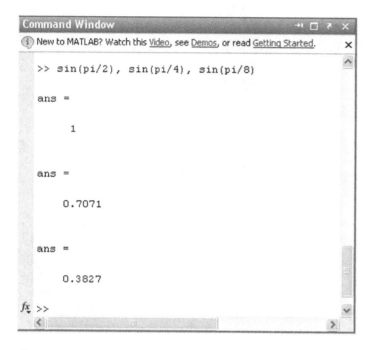

Figure 1-14.

It is possible to enter descriptive comments in a command input line starting them with the "%" sign. When you run the input, MATLAB ignores the comment area and processes the rest.

```
>> L = log (123)

L =

    4.8122
```

To simplify the process of the introduction of scripts to be evaluated by the interpreter of MATLAB (via the Command Window), you can use the arrow computer keys to access the command history. For example, if you press the up arrow once, we recover the last entry submitted in MATLAB. If you press the key up twice, it recovers the penultimate entry submitted, and so on.

If you type a sequence of characters in the *input* area and then click the up arrow, MATLAB recovers the last entry that begins with the specified string.

Commands entered during a MATLAB session are temporarily stored in the buffer (*Workspace*) until you end the session with the program, at which time they can be permanently stored in a file or you lose them permanently.

Below is a summary of the keys that can be used in the area of *input* of MATLAB (command line), as well as its functions:

Up arrow (Ctrl-P)	Retrieves the previous line. Opens the print dialog
Arrow down (Ctrl-N)	Retrieves the following entry. Creates a new file in the Editor.
Arrow to the left (Ctrl-B)	Takes the cursor to the left one character.
Arrow to the right (Ctrl-F)	Takes the cursor to the right one character. Performs a search/find that opens a dialog.
CTRL-arrow to the left	Takes the cursor to the start of the word or to the start of the word to the left.
CTRL-arrow to the right	Takes the cursor to the end of the current word or the end of the word to the right.
Home (Ctrl-A)	Takes the cursor to the beginning of the line.
End (Ctrl-E)	Takes the cursor to the end of the current line.
Escape	Clears the command line.
Delete (Ctrl-D)	Deletes the character at the right of the cursor.
BACKSPACE	Deletes the character to the left of the cursor.
CTRL-K	Deletes all of the rest of the current line.

The command *clc* clears the Command Window, but it does not delete the variables of the work area (that content remains in memory).

1.3 Help in MATLAB

MATLAB help through the help button in the toolbar can be accessed here 🔵 or through the *Help* menu bar option. In addition, support can also be obtained through commands implemented as MATLAB objects. The command *help* provides general help on all commands in MATLAB (Figure 1-15). By clicking on any of them, you get your particular help. For example, if you click on the hyperlink *graph2d*, you get support for graphics in two dimensions (Figure 1-16).

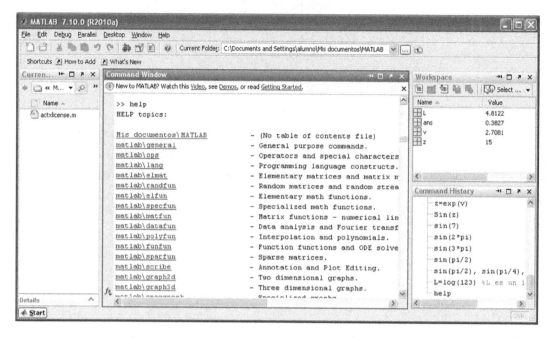

Figure 1-15.

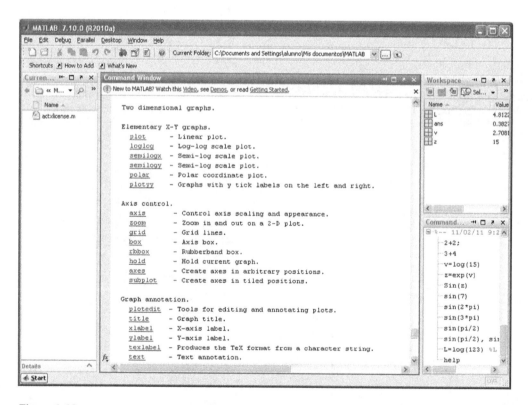

Figure 1-16.

You can ask for help on a specific command (Figure 1-17) or on any subject content (Figure 1-18) using the command *help command* or *help topic*.

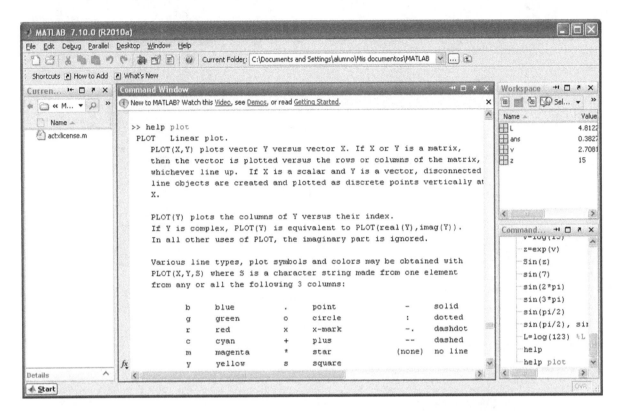

Figure 1-17.

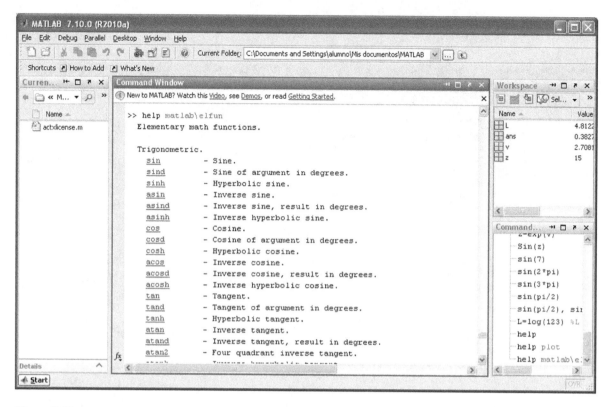

Figure 1-18.

The command string *lookfor* allows you to find all those functions or commands of MATLAB that refer to your sequence or contain it. This command is very useful, to view all commands that contain the sequence. For example, if we seek help for all commands that contain the sequence *investor*, can use the command *lookfor investor* (Figure 1-19).

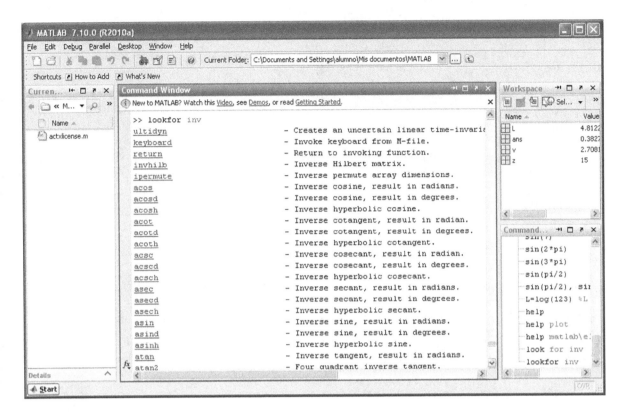

Figure 1-19.

1.4 Numerical Calculations with MATLAB

You can use MATLAB as a powerful numerical calculator. Most calculators handle numbers only with a preset degree of precision, however MATLAB performs exact calculations with necessary precision. In addition, unlike calculators, we can perform operations not only with individual numbers, but also with objects such as arrays.

Most of the themes of the classical numerical calculations, are treated in this software. It supports matrix calculations, statistics, interpolation, fit by least squares, numerical integration, minimization of functions, linear programming, numerical algebraic and resolution of differential equations and a long list of processes of numerical analysis that we'll see later in this book.

Here are some examples of numerical calculations with MATLAB. (As we all know, for results it is necessary to press Enter once you have written the corresponding expressions next to the prompt ">>")

We can simply calculate 4 + 3 and get as a result 7. To do this, just type 4 + 3, and then Enter.

>> 4 + 3

Ans =

7

Also we can get the value of 3 to the 100th power, without having previously set precision. For this purpose press 3 ^ 100.

```
>> 3 ^ 100
```

Ans =

5. 1538e + 047

You can use the command "format long e" to return the result of the operation with 16 digits before the exponent (scientific notation).

```
>> format long e
```

```
>> 3^100
```

ans =

5.153775207320115e+047

we also can work with complex numbers. We will get the result of the operation (2 + 3i) raised to the 10th power, by typing the expression (2 + 3i) ^ 10.

```
>> (2 + 3i) ^ 10
```

Ans =

-1 415249999999998e + 005 - 1. 456680000000000e + 005i

(5) The previous result is also available in short format, using the "format short" command.

```
>> format short
>> (2 + 3i)^10
```

ans =

-1.4152e+005- 1.4567e+005i

Also we can calculate the value of the Bessel function found in section 11.5. To do this type Besselj (0,11.5).

```
>> besselj(0,11.5)
```

ans =

-0.0677

1.5 Symbolic Calculations with MATLAB

MATLAB handles symbolic mathematical computation using the Symbolic Math Toolbox, manipulating formulae and algebraic expressions easily and quickly and can perform most operations with them. You can expand, factor and simplify polynomials, rational and trigonometric expressions, you can find algebraic solutions of polynomial equations and systems of equations, can evaluate derivatives and integrals symbolically, and find function solutions for differential equations, you can manipulate powers, limits and many other facets of algebraic mathematical series.

To perform this task, MATLAB requires all the variables (or algebraic expressions) to be written between single quotes to distinguish them from numerical solutions. When MATLAB receives a variable or expression in quotes, it is considered symbolic.

Here are some examples of symbolic computation with MATLAB.

1. You can raise the following algebraic expression to the third power: $(x + 1) (x+2) - (x+2)^2$.
    This is done by typing the following expression: expand $('((x + 1) (x+2) - (x+2)^2)^3')$.
    The result will be another algebraic expression:

    ```
    >> syms x; expand (((x + 1) *(x + 2)-(x + 2) ^ 2) ^ 3)
    ```

    Ans =

    $-x^3-6*x^2-12*x-8$

    Note that syms x is used to declare x for symbolic computations.
    You can then factor the result of the calculation in the example above by typing:
    factor $('((x+1)*(x+2)-(x+2)^2)^3')$

    ```
    >> syms x; factor(((x + 1)*(x + 2)-(x + 2)^2)^3)
    ```

    ans =

    $-(x+2)^3$

2. You can resolve the indefinite integral of the function $(x^2) Sine (x)^2$ by typing:
    int $('x^2 * \sin(x)^2', 'x')$

    ```
    >> int('x^2*sin(x)^2', 'x')
    ```

    ans =

    $x^2 * (-1/2 * \cos(x) * \sin(x) + 1/2 * x)-1/2 * x * \cos(x)^2 + 1/4 * \cos(x) * \sin(x) + 1/4 * 1/x-3 * x^3$

    You can simplify the previous result:

    ```
    >> syms x; simplify(int(x^2*sin(x)^2, x))
    ```

    ans =

    $\sin(2*x)/8 - (x*\cos(2*x))/4 - (x^2*\sin(2*x))/4 + x^3/6$

You can express the previous result with more elegant mathematical notation:

```
>> syms x; pretty(simplify(int(x^2*sin(x)^2, x)))
```

$$\frac{\sin(2\ x)}{8} - \frac{x\ \cos(2\ x)}{4} - \frac{x^2\ \sin(2\ x)}{4} + \frac{x^3}{6}$$

3. We can solve the equation $3ax - 7x^2 + x^3 = 0$ (where a, is a parameter):

```
>> solve('3*a*x-7*x^2 + x^3 = 0', 'x')
```

ans =

```
[                        0]
[7/2 + 1/2 *(49-12*a) ^(1/2)]
[7/2 - 1/2 *(49-12*a) ^(1/2)]
```

4. We can find the five solutions of the equation $x^5 + 2x + 1 = 0$:

ans =

```
                              -0.48638903593454300001655725369801
    0.94506808682313338631496614476119 + 0.85451751443904587692179191887616*i
    0.94506808682313338631496614476119 - 0.85451751443904587692179191887616*i
  - 0.70187356885586188630668751791218 - 0.87969719792982402287026727381769*i
  - 0.70187356885586188630668751791218 + 0.87969719792982402287026727381769*i
```

As mentioned before, MATLAB can be extended by utilizing other libraries to extend its functionality. In particular, MATLAB may use the libraries of the Maple V program, to work with symbolic math and can thus extend its field of action. In this way, you can use MATLAB to work on issues such as differential forms, Euclidean geometry, projective geometry, statistics, etc.

At the same time, you also can expand the topics of numerical calculation, using the libraries from MATLAB and libraries of Maple (combinatorics, optimization, theory of numbers, etc.)

1.6 Graphics with MATLAB

MATLAB produces graphs of two and three dimensions, as well as outlines and graphics of density. You can represent the graphics and list the data. MATLAB allows you to control colors, shading and other graphics features, also supports animated graphics. Graphics produced by MATLAB are portable to other programs.

Here are some examples of MATLAB graphics:

1. You can represent the function xSine (x) for x ranging between $-\pi/4$ and $\pi/4$ taking 300 equidistant points for the intervals. See Figure 1-20.

```
>> x = linspace(-pi/4,pi/4,300);
>> y = x.*sin(1./x);
>> plot(x,y)0
```

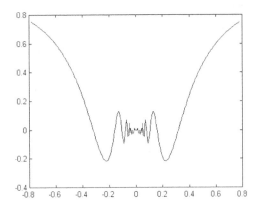

Figure 1-20.

2. You can give the graph above the options frame and grille, as well create your own chart title and labels for axes. See Figure 1-21.

```
>> x = linspace(-pi/4,pi/4,300);
>> y = x.*sin(1./x);
>> plot(x,y);
>> grid;
>> xlabel('Independent variable X');
>> ylabel ('Independent variable Y');
>> title ('The function y=xsin(1/x)')
```

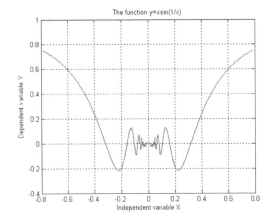

Figure 1-21.

3. You can generate a graph of the surface for the function z = Sin (sqrt(x^2+y^2)) / sqrt(x^2+y^2), making the variables (also axes) x and y span the range of -7.5 to +7.5 in 0.5 increments. See Figure 1-22.

```
>> x =-7.5:.5:7.5;
>> y = x;
>> [X, Y] = meshgrid(x,y);
>> Z = sin(sqrt(X.^2+Y.^2))./sqrt(X.^2+Y.^2);
>> surf (X, Y, Z)
```

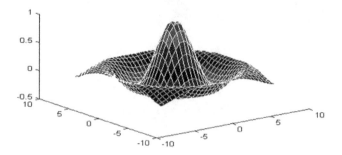

Figure 1-22.

These 3D graphics allow you to get an idea of the figures in space, and are very helpful in visually identifying intersections between different bodies, generation of developments of all kinds and volumes of revolution.

4. You can generate a three dimensional graphic corresponding to the Helix in parametric coordinates: x = Sin (t), y = Cos(t), z = t. See Figure 1-23.

```
>> t = 0:pi/50:10*pi;
>> plot3(sin(t),cos(t),t)
```

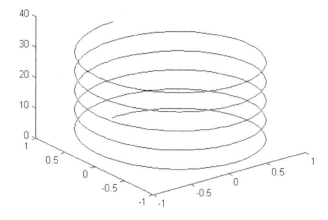

Figure 1-23.

24

5. We can represent a planar curve given by its polar coordinates r = Cos (2t) * Sine (2t) for t varying between 0 and π, taking equally spaced points in one-hundredths of the considered range. See Figure 1-24.

```
>> t = 0:.1:2 * pi;
>> r = sin(2*t).* cos(2*t);
>> polar(t,r)
```

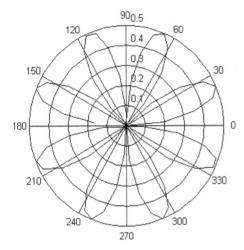

Figure 1-24.

6. We can also make a graph of a function considered as symbolic, using the command "ezplot". See Figure 1-25.

```
>> y ='x ^ 3 /(x^2-1)';
>> ezplot(y,[-5,5])
```

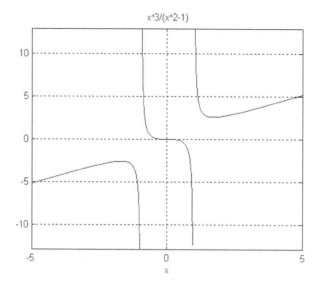

$x^3/(x^2-1)$

Figure 1-25.

In the corresponding chapter of graphics we will extend these concepts.

1.7 MATLAB and Programming

Programs usually consist of a series of instructions in which values are calculated, are assigned a name or value and are reused in further calculations.

As in programming languages like C or Fortran, in MATLAB you can write programs with loops, control flow and conditionals. In MATLAB you can write procedural programs, i.e., to define a sequence of standard steps to run. As in C or Pascal, a Do, For, or While may be used for repetitive calculations to be performed. The language of MATLAB also includes conditional constructs such as If Then Else. MATLAB also supports different logic functions, such as And, Or, Not and Xor.

MATLAB supports procedural programming (iterative, recursive, loops...), functional programming and object-oriented programming. Here are two simple examples of programs. For our purposes, he first generates the order n Hilbert matrix (which can also be gotten by using hilb(n), and the second calculates the Fibonacci numbers for values less than 1000.

```
% Generating the order n Hilbert matrix
t = '1/(i+j-1)';
for i = 1:n
for j = 1:n
a(i,j) = eval(t);
end
end

% Calculating Fibonacci numbers
f = [1 2 3]
i = 1;
while f(i) + f(i-1) < 1000
f(i+2) = f(i) + f(i+1);
i = i+1;
end
```

Two-Dimensional Graphics. Statistics Graphics and Curves in Explicit, Parametric and Polar Coordinates

MATLAB allows the representation of any mathematical function, even if it is defined piecewise or jumps to infinity in its field of definition. MATLAB makes graphs of planar (two-dimensional) curves and surfaces (three-dimensional), groups them and can overlap them. You can combine colors, grids, frames, etc., in the graphics. MATLAB allows representations of functions in implicit, explicit and parametric coordinates, and is without a doubt mathematical software with high graphics performance. One of their differences with the rest of the symbolic calculation packages is that "animations" can be generated by combining different graphics with slight variations from each other displayed quickly in succession, to give the impression of movement generated from graphs similarly to moving pictures and cartoons.

In addition, MATLAB also allows for typical bar graphs, lines, star graphs and histograms. It also offers special possibilities of representation of polyhedra with geographical maps. In handling of graphics, it is very important to bear in mind the availability of memory on the computer. The graphics drawings consume lots of memory and require high screen resolution.

2.1 Two-Dimensional Graphics (2-D)

The basic commands that MATLAB uses to draw the graph of a function of a variable are as follows:

plot(X,Y) draws the set of points (X, Y), where X and Y are row vectors. For graphing a function $y = f(x)$, it is necessary to know a set of points $(X, f(X))$, to set a range of variation for the vector X. X and Y can be matrices of the same size, in which case a graph is made by plotting each pair of rows and on the same axis. For complex values of X and Y, the imaginary parts are ignored.

plot (Y) draws the vector Y elements, i.e., gives the graph of the set of points (t, Y_t) for $t = 1, 2,... n$ where $n = length (Y)$. It is useful for graphing time series. If Y is a matrix, plot (Y) makes a graph for each column Y presenting all on the same axis. If the components of the vector are complex, $plot (Y)$ is equivalent to $plot (real (Y), imag (Y))$.

plot (X, Y, S) draws *plot(X,Y)* with the settings defined in *S*. Usually, *S* consists of two symbols between single quotes, the first of which sets the color of the line of the graph, and the second sets the character to be used in the plotting. The possible values of colors and characters are, respectively, as follows:

```
y yellow      .  Point marker
m magenta     o  Circle marker
c cyan        x  X marker
r Red         +  Plus signs
g green       -  Solid line
b Blue        *  Star marker
w White       :  Dotted line
k Black       -. Dashes and dots
              -  Dashed line
```

plot(X1,Y1,S1,X2,Y2,S2,X3,Y3,S3,...) combines, on the same axes, graphs defined for the triplets *(Xi, Yi, Si)*. It is a way of representing various functions on the same graph.

fplot(function, [xmin, *x*max]) graphs the function for the variation of *x* over the given range.

fplot(function, [xmin, *x*max, ymin, ymax], S) graphs the function over the range xmin to xmax while limiting the y-axis to the range of ymin to ymax, with options for color, line style, and markers given by S.

fplot([f1,f2,...,fn],[xmin, *x*max, ymin, ymax], S) graphs functions *f1, f2,..., fn* on the same axes at intervals for the range of *x* and *y* specified, and the color, line, and marker styles defined in *S*.

ezplot ('expression', [xmin *x*max]) graphs the expression for the variation of *x* given in the range.

Let's see some examples of 2-dimensional graphics:
We will begin by representing the function $f(x) = (sin(x))^2 + 2xcos(x)$ (-2,2):

```
>> x = [-2*pi:0.1:2*pi];
>> y = sin(x) .^ 2 + 2 * x .* cos(x);
>> plot(x,y)
```

MATLAB returns the graph that is shown in Figure 2-1. It is worth noting that the definition of the function has been made in vector form, using the notation for vector variables. The range of the trigonometric function is defined in pi radian (in this case -2 pi to 2 pi).

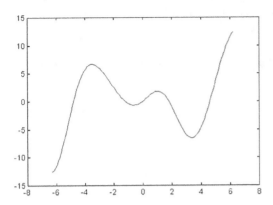

Figure 2-1.

The same graph is obtained using the command *fplot* with the following syntax:

```
>> fplot ('sin(x) ^ 2 + 2 * x * cos(x)', [- 2 * pi, 2 * pi])
```

And the same representation can be obtained by using the command ***ezplot*** using the following syntax:

```
>> ezplot ('sin(x) ^ 2 + 2 * x * cos(x)', [- 2 * pi, 2 * pi])
```

Observe that in the last two cases functions are expressed symbolically, and not as a vector, as in the form of the first case. (Note the quotes surrounding the function).

MATLAB draws not only bounded functions, but it also represents features that have asymptotes and singularities. For example, Figure 2-2 shows the graph of the function $y = x^3/(x^2-4)$ which has asymptotes for x at -2 and 2 in the range of variation of *x* given by *(- 8,8)* by using the command:

```
>> ezplot ('x ^ 3 / (x^2-4)', [- 8, 8])
```

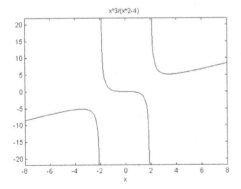

Figure 2-2.

29

EXERCISE 2-1

Represent the graphs of the functions *Sine(x)*, *Sine(2x)* and *Sine(3x)*, varying in the range (0,2π) for *x*, all on the same axes.

The graphics, generated by the input is represented in Figure 2-3:

```
fplot (@(x)[sin(x), sin(2*x), sin(3*x)], [0, 2 * pi])
```

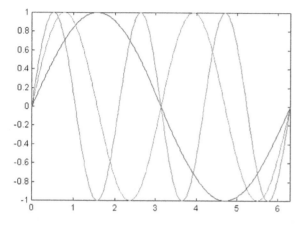

Figure 2-3.

It may be useful to differentiate between curves by their strokes, for instance if you cannot assume that your ultimate user of the graph can print in color. For variety, in Figure 2-4 we represent the first function, *Sine (x)*, with a black line, the second, *Sine(2x)*, using blue star, and the third, *Sine (3x)*, with red circles. We use the following syntax:

```
>> x = (0:0.05:2*pi);
>> y1 = sin(x); y2 = sin(2*x); y3 = sin(3*x);
>> plot(x,y1,'k-',x,y2,'b*',x,y3,'ro')
```

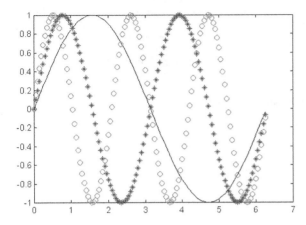

Figure 2-4.

2.2 Titles, Tags, Meshes and Texts

The commands available in MATLAB for these purposes are as follows:

title ('text') adds the text used as the title of the graph at the Top in 2-D and 3-D graphics.

xlabel ('text') places the text next to the *x* axis in 2-D and 3-D graphics.

ylabel ('text') puts the text next to the y axis in 2-D and 3-D graphics.

zlabel ('text') places the text beside axis *z* in a 3-D chart.

text (x, y, 'text') places the text at the point *(x, y)* within the 2-D chart.

text (x, y, z, 'text') places the text at the point *(x, y, z)* in a 3D graphic.

gtext ('text') allows you to place text at a point selected with the mouse within a 2-D chart.

grid locates grids in a 2-D or 3-D chart axes. The command *grid on* places the major grid lines and *grid off* removes them. The *grid* command without a parameter toggles the grid between *on* and *off*. The command *hold* keeps the current graph with all its properties, so that subsequent graphs are placed on the same axis overlapping the existing one. The option *hold on* activates the option and *hold off* deletes the option. The *hold* command without a parameter toggles between *on* and *off*. Axis autoranging behavior is not affected by the *hold* command.

EXERCISE 2-2

On the same axes represent the graphs of the functions $y = sin\ (x^2)$ and $y = log\ (sqrt\ (x))$. The text of each equation is properly positioned within the graph.

We get the graph in Figure 2-5 considering the following MATLAB entry:

```
>> x = linspace (0,2,30);
>> y = sin(x.^2);
>> plot(x,y)
>> text (1,0.8, ' y = sin(x^2)')
>> hold on
>> z = log(sqrt(x));
>> plot (x, z)
>> text (1, - 0.1, ' y = log (sqrt (x))')
>> xlabel('X Axis');
>> ylabel ('Y Axis');
>> title('Graphic sine and logarithmic');
```

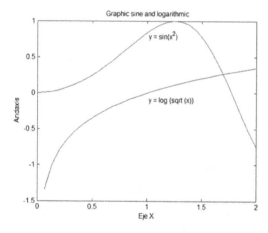

Figure 2-5.

2.3 Manipulating Graphics

Below, are commands that allow you to manipulate the axes of a graph, placement of it within the screen, their appearance, their presentation from different points of view, etc.

axis([xmin *x*max ymin ymax]) assigns the minimum and maximum values for the X and Y axes in the graphic.

axis('auto') assigns scaling for each axis based upon the actual range of values represented in the plot, which is the default mode i.e., xmin=min(x), xmax=max(x), ymin=min(y), ymax=max(y)

axis('manual') freezes the scaling of axes to the current settings, so that limits from placing other graphs on the same axes (with *hold* in *on*), do not change the scale.

V = axis gives the vector V of 4 elements the scale of the current graph is [xmin xmax ymin ymax].

axis('xy') places the graph in Cartesian coordinate mode, which is the default, with the origin at the bottom left of the graph.

axis('ij') sets the graph to matrix coordinate mode, where the origin is at the top left of the graph, with i being the vertical axis increasing from top to bottom and j being the horizontal axis increasing from left to right.

axis('square') the plotted rectangle becomes a square, so the figures will absorb the change in scale.

axis('equal') makes the aspect ratio for all axes the same.

axis('normal') eliminates the options *square* and *equal.*

axis('off') eliminates labels and brands on the axes and grids, keeping the title of the chart and the text applied using *text* with *gtext.*

axis('on') restores labels, marks and axes grids.

subplot (m, n, p) divides the graphics window in *m x n* subwindows and places the current graphic window in the*p-th position*, beginning the count from the left top and from left to right; then it goes to the next line until it is finished. For example, if m=3 and n=2 then p is expected to be used with values between 1 and 6, with plots 1 and 2 being in the first row, 3 and 4 in the second, and 5 and 6 in the third row.

EXERCISE 2-3

Present in the same figure the graphs of the functions *Sin(x)* and *Cos (x)*, placed horizontally one next to each other with their names, with the *x* axis values between 0 and 2 * pi, a shaft, and taking *y* values between - 1 and 1. Also get the vertical representation, so that they one under the other and use slotted shafts.

MATLAB, we propose the following entry:

```
>> x = (0:0.1:2*pi);
>> y = sin(x);
>> z = cos(x);
>> subplot(1,2,1);
>> plot(x,y), axis([0, 2*pi, -1, 1]), title('sin(x)')
>> subplot(1,2,2);
>> plot(x,z), axis([0, 2*pi, -1, 1]), title('cos(x)')
```

The result is presented in Figure 2-6:

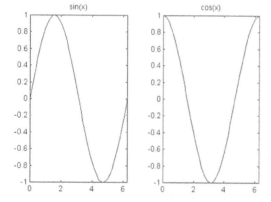

Figure 2-6.

We now propose to MATLAB the following entry to shift the Sine curve to the top:

```
>> x = (0:0.1:4*pi);
>> y = sin (x);
>> z = cos (x);
>> subplot(2,1,1);
>> plot(x,y), axis([0 2*pi -1 1]), title('sin(x)'), grid
>> subplot(2,1,2);
>> plot (x, z), axis([0 2*pi -1 1]), title ('cos (x)'), grid
```

The result is presented in Figure 2-7:

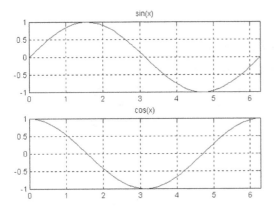

Figure 2-7.

EXERCISE 2-4

Present in the same figure, graphs of the functions *Sine (x), Cos (x), Cosec (x)* and *Sec (x)*, placed in a matrix of four graphics, but under each function place its inverse for *x* ranging from [- 2π, 2π].

We use the command *subplot* to draw the four functions, in the appropriate order under *Sine (x)* place *Cosec (x)*, and under *Cos (x)*, place *Sec (x)*. The syntax will be as follows:

```
>> subplot(2,2,1);
>> ezplot('sin (x)', [- 2 * pi, 2 * pi])
>> subplot(2,2,2);
>> ezplot('cos(x)',[-2*pi 2*pi])
>> subplot(2,2,3);
>> ezplot('csc(x)',[-2*pi 2*pi])
>> subplot(2,2,4);
>> ezplot('sec(x)',[-2*pi 2*pi])
```

MATLAB offers as a result the graph of Figure 2-8.

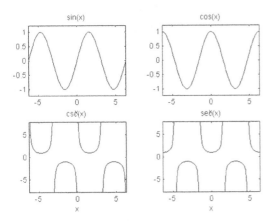

Figure 2-8.

2.4 Logarithmic Graphics

The commands that enable MATLAB to represent graphs with logarithmic scales are the following:

loglog(X,Y) performs the same graphics as *plot(X,Y)*, but with logarithmic scales on the two axes. This command presents the same variants and supports the same options as the command *plot*.

semilogx(X,Y) performs the same graphics as *plot(X,Y)*, but with logarithmic scale on the *x* axis, and normal scale on the y axis (semilogarithmic scale).

semilogy(X,Y) performs the same graphics as *plot(X,Y)*, but with logarithmic scale on the y axis and normal scale on the *x* axis (semilogarithmic scale).

EXERCISE 2-5

Present on the same graph the function $y = abs(e^{-1/2} \times Sine(5x))$ represented in normal scale, logarithmic scale and semilogarithmic scales.

The syntax presented here leads us to Figure 2-9, which compares the graph of the same function for the different scales. The graph is represented in the upper part with normal and logarithmic scales and at the bottom, the two semilogarithmic scales.

```
>> x = 0:0.01:3;
>> y = abs(exp(-0.5*x) .* sin(5*x));
>> subplot(2,2,1)
>> plot(x,y)
>> title('normal')
>> hold on
>> subplot(2,2,2)
>> loglog(x,y)
>> title('logarithmic')
>> subplot(2,2,3)
>> semilogx(x,y)
>> title('semilogarithmic in X axis')
>> subplot(2,2,4)
>> semilogy(x,y)
>> title('semilogarithmic in Y axis')
```

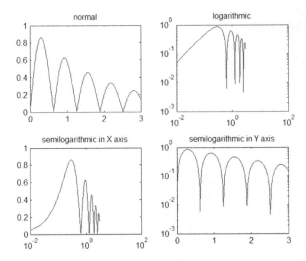

Figure 2-9.

2.5 Polygons

MATLAB also allows drawing polygons in two dimensions. To do this, use the following commands:

fill(X, Y, C) draws the compact polygon whose vertices are pairs of coordinates *(Xi, Yi)* of the column vectors *X* and *Y*. If C is a vector of the same size of *X* and *Y*, it contains the color map index *Ci* for each point *(Xi, Yi) as scaled by c axis*. If C is a single character, all the points of the polygon will be painted the color corresponding to the character. The *Ci* values may be: *'r', 'g', 'b', 'c', ', 'y', 'w', 'k'*, whose meanings we already know. If *X* and *Y* are matrices of the same size, several polygons will be represented at the same time corresponding to each pair of column vectors *(X.j, Y.j)*. In this case, C can be a vector row *Cj* elements determine the unique color of each pair of vectors for polygon column *(X.j, Y.j)*. C can also be a matrix of the same dimension as *X* and Y, in which case its elements determine the color of each point *(Xij, Yij)* in the set of polygons.

fill(X1,Y1,C1,X2,Y2,C2,...) draws multiple compact polygons whose vertices are given by the points *(Xi, Yi, Ci)*, the meaning of which we already know.

EXERCISE 2-6

Represent a regular octagon (square enclosure), whose vertices are defined by pairs of values *(Sine (t), Cos (t))*, for values of *t* varying between 8π and 15π/8 separated by 2π/8. Use only the green color and put the 'Octagon' text at the point (-1/4,0) the inside of the figure.

The syntax for Figure 2-10 is the following:

```
>> t = [pi/8:2*pi/8:15*pi/8]';
>> x = sin (t);
>> y = cos (t);
>> fill(x,y,'g')
>> axis('square')
>> text(-0.25,0,'OCTOGON)'
```

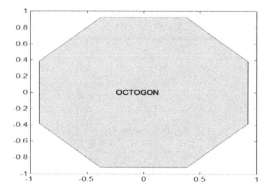

Figure 2-10.

2.6 Graphics Functions in Parametric Coordinates 2-D

We are going to see now how the program draws curves in parametric coordinates in the plane. We will discuss how you can get graphs of functions in which the variables *x* and *y* depend, in turn, on a parameter *t*. The command to use is *Plot* and all its variants, conveniently defining intervals of the parameter variation, and not the independent variable, as it was until now.

EXERCISE 2-7

Represent the curve (Epicycloid) whose parametric coordinates are: $x = 4Cos\ [t] - Cos\ [4t]$, $y = 4Sine\ [t] - Sine\ [4t]$, for t varying between 0 and 2π.

The syntax will be as follows:

```
>> t = 0:0.01:2 * pi;
>> x = 4 * cos (t) - cos(4*t);
>> y = 4 * sin (t) - sin(4*t);
>> plot(x,y)
```

The graph is presented in Figure 2-11, and represents the **epicycloid**.

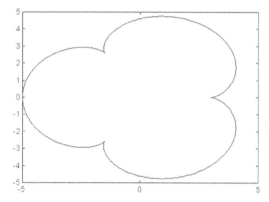

Figure 2-11.

EXERCISE 2-8

Represent the graph of the Cycloid whose parametric equations are $x = t-2Sine\ (t)$, $y = 1-2Cos\ (t)$, for t varying between -3π. and 3π.

We will use the following syntax:

```
>> t = - 3 * pi:0.001:3 * pi;
>> plot(t-2 * sin (t), 1-2 * cos (t))
```

This gives you the graph in Figure 2-12.

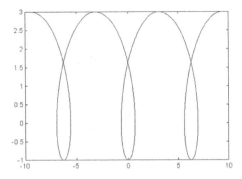

Figure 2-12.

2.7 Graphics Functions in Polar Coordinates

MATLAB enables the specific *polar* command, representing functions in polar coordinates. Its syntax is as follows:

Polar (α, r) represents the curve in polar coordinates $r = r(\alpha)$, *using theta in radians.*

Polar (α, r, S) represents the curve in polar coordinates $r = r(\alpha)$ with the style of line given by S, whose values were already specified in the command *plot*.

EXERCISE 2-9

Represent the graph of the curve whose equation in polar coordinates is as follows: $r = Sine\ (2a)\ Cos\ (2a)$ for a between 0 and 2π.

The following syntax leads us to the graph in Figure 2-13:

```
>> a = 0:0.01:2 * pi;
>> r = sin(2*a)   .* cos(2*a);
>> polar(a, r)
```

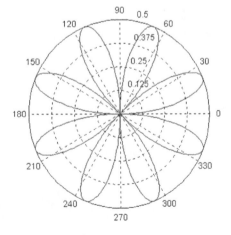

Figure 2-13.

40

EXERCISE 2-10

Represent the graph of the curve whose equation in polar coordinates is as follows: $r = 4 (1 + Cos (a))$ for a between 0 and 2π, (called a cardioid).

To get the graph of Figure 2-14, representing the cardioid, use the following syntax:

```
>> a = 0:0.01:2 * pi;
>> r = 4 * (1 + cos (a));
>> polar(a, r)
>> title('CARDIOID')
```

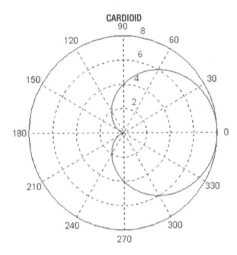

Figure 2-14.

EXERCISE 2-11

Represent the graph of the Lemniscate of Bernoulli whose equation is $r = 4 (cos (2a) \wedge (1/2))$ for 0 and 2, and the graph of the spiral of Archimedes whose equation is $r = 3a, \quad -4\pi < a < -4\pi$.

The first curve is represented in Figure 2-15, and is obtained by the following syntax:

```
>> a = 0:0.01:2 * pi;
>> r = 4 * (cos(2*a).^(1/2));
>> polar(a, r)
>> title(' Lemniscate of Bernoulli ')
```

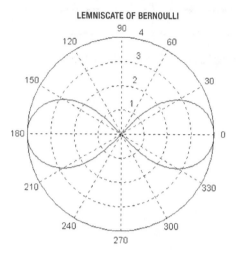

Figure 2-15.

The second curve is represented in Figure 2-16, and is obtained by the following syntax:

```
>> a = -4 * pi:0.01*pi:4 * pi;
>> r = 3 * a;
>> polar(a, r)
>> title('spiral of ARCHIMEDES')
```

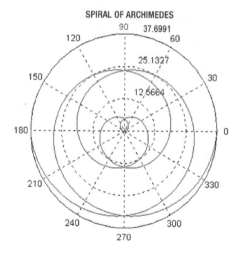

Figure 2-16.

2.8 Bars and Sectors Graphics. Histograms

MATLAB constructs bar graphs, sectors, Pareto diagrams and histograms of frequencies through the following commands:

bar(Y) draws a bar graph relative to the vector of magnitudes *Y*.

bar(X,Y) draws a bar graph on the vector of magnitudes *Y* whose elements are given by the vector *X*.

stairs (Y) draws the staggered step graph relative to the vector *Y*.

stairs(X,Y) draws the ladder graph relative to the vector *Y* whose elements are given by the vector *X*.

hist(Y) draws a histogram using 10 vertical rectangles of equal base relative to the Y vector frequencies.

hist(Y,n) draws a histogram using vertical rectangles of equal base relative to the Y vector frequencies.

hist(Y,X) draws a histogram, using vertical rectangles whose bin center values are specified in the elements of the vector *X*, relative to the *Y* vector frequencies.

foot(X) draws the pie chart relative to the *X* vector frequencies.

pie(X,Y) draws the pie chart relative to the *X* vector frequency leaving out the sectors in which Yi<0.

pareto(X) draws the Pareto graph relative to the vector *X*.

Here are some examples:

```
>> bar([1 - 3, 4, 5, 2, 3])
>> pie([1, 3, 4, 5, 2, 3])
```

The graphics are in Figures 2-17 and 2-18.

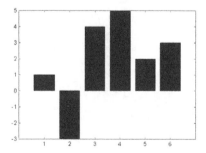

Figure 2-17.

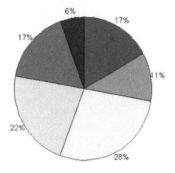

Figure 2-18.

Below, is a bar chart for 20 values of a normal between - 3 and 3:

```
>> x = -3:0.3:3;
>> bar(x, exp(-x.^2))
```

This generates the graph in Figure 2-19.

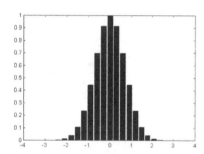

Figure 2-19.

Figure 2-20 represents the step graph corresponding to the previous bar graph whose syntax is:

```
>> x = -3:0.3:3;
>> stairs(x,exp(-x.^2))
```

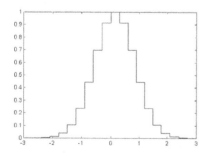

Figure 2-20.

44

The histogram in Figure 2-21, corresponds to a vector of 10,000 normal random values in 60 bins between the values - 3 and 3 in0.1 increments:

```
>> x = -3:0.1:3;
>> y = randn(10000,1);
>> hist(y,x)
```

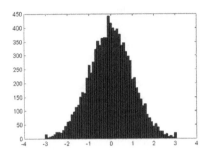

Figure 2-21.

Figure 2-22 is a pie chart with two of its areas displaced, produced by using the syntax:

```
>> pie([1, 3, 4, 5, 2, 3], [0,0,0,0,1,1])
```

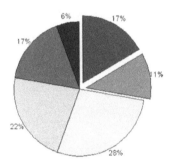

Figure 2-22.

2.9 Statistical Errors and Arrow Graphics

There are commands in MATLAB which enable charting errors of a function, as well as certain types of arrow graphics to be discussed now. Some of these commands are described below:

errorbar(x,y,e) carries out the graph of the vector *x* against the vector *y* with the errors specified in the vector *e*. Passing through each point *(xi, yi)* draws a vertical line of length 2ei whose center is the point *(xi, yi)*.

stem(Y) draws the graph of the vector *Y* cluster. Each point *Y* is attached to the axis *x* by a vertical line.

stem(X,Y) draw the graph of the *Y* vector cluster whose elements are given by the vector *X*.

rose(Y) draws the angular histogram relative to the vector *and* angles in radians, using 20 equal radii.

rose(Y,n) draws the vector *Y* angular histogram, *using equal radii.*

rose(X,Y) draws the vector *Y angular* histogram using radii that are specified in the elements of the vector *X.*

compass(Z) carries out a diagram of arrows coming out of the origin and whose magnitude and direction are determined by the real and imaginary components of the vector *Z* in complex numbers. The complex *Zi* arrow joins the origin with the value of *Zi.*

compass(X,Y) is equivalent to *compass (X+i*Y).*

compass (Z, S) or **compass(X, Y, S)** specifies the line type in *S* to use on the arrows.

feather(Z) or **feather(X,Y)** or **feather(Z,S)** or **feather(X,Y,S)** is the same as *compass*, with the only difference that the origin of the arrows is not at the origin of coordinates, but out of equally-spaced points of a horizontal line.

legend('legend1', 'legend2',..., 'legendn') situates the legends given in *n* consecutive graphics.

Here are some examples below:

First of all, let's represent in Figure 2-23 a chart of errors for the density of a normal distribution (0,1) function, with the variable defined in 40 points between - 4 and 4, and errors are being defined by 40 uniform random values (0.10):

```
>> x  = -4:.2:4;
>> y = (1/sqrt(2*pi))*exp(-(x.^2)/2);
>> e = rand(size(x))/10;
>> errorbar(x,y,e)
```

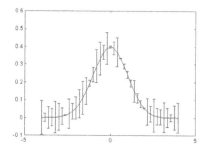

Figure 2-23.

We also represent a graph of clusters corresponding to 50 normal random numbers (0.1) by using the syntax below in Figure 2-24:

```
>> y = randn (50,1); stem (y)
```

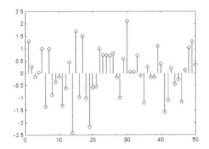

Figure 2-24.

Figure 2-25 is an angular histogram with 1,000 a multiples of as a reason for normal random multiplicity (0.1), obtained from the following syntax:

```
>> x = 0:0.1:2 * pi;
>> y = randn (1000,1) * pi;
>> rose(y,x)
```

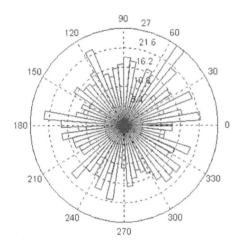

Figure 2-25.

Now, Figure 2-26 presents a chart of arrows with center at the origin, corresponding to the eigenvalues of a normal (0,1) random square matrix of size 20 x 20. The syntax is as follows:

```
>> z = eig(randn (20,20));
>> compass(z)
```

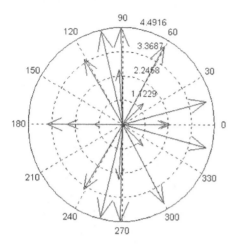

Figure 2-26.

Figure 2-27 is going to represent the chart of arrows in the previous example, but with the origin of the arrows in a horizontal straight line. The syntax is:

```
>> z = eig(randn (20,20));
>> feather(z)
```

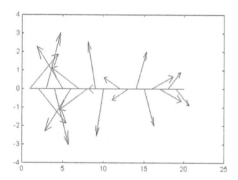

Figure 2-27.

Finally, we will draw on the same axes (Figure 2-28) the *bessel(1,x)*,*bessel(2,x)*y *bessel(3,x)* functions for values of *x* between 0 and 12, separated uniformly in two-tenths. The purpose of the chart is to place three legends and three different types of stroke (normal, asterisks and circles, respectively) to the three functions. The syntax will be as follows:

```
>> x = 0:0.2:12;
>> plot (x, besselj(1,x), x, besselj(2,x),'*g', x, besselj(3,x), 'dr');
>> legend('Bessel(1,x)','Bessel(2,x)','Bessel(3,x)');
```

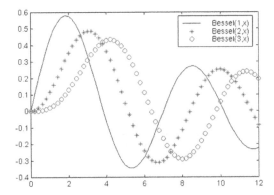

Figure 2-28.

CHAPTER 3

■ ■ ■

Three-Dimensional Graphics, Warped Curves and Surfaces, Contour Graphics

3.1 Three-Dimensional Graphics (3-D), Warped Curves

The basic commands that MATLAB uses to draw graphs that generate a line in three dimensions or **warped curves** are the following:

plot3(X, Y, Z) draws the set of points *(X, Y, Z)*, where *X*, *Y* and *Z* are vectors. *X*, Y and Z can also be arrays of the same size, in which case a graph is made for each triplet of rows and on the same axis. For complex values of *X*, *Y* and *Z*, the imaginary parts are ignored.

plot3(X,Y,Z,S) draws the plot (X, Y, Z) with the settings defined in *S*. Usually *S* consists of two-symbols between single quotes, the first of which sets the color of the line of the graph, and the second sets the character to be used in the plotting. The possible values of colors and characters have been already described to explain the command *plot*.

plot3(X1,Y1,Z1,S1,X2,Y2,Z2,S2,X3,Y3,Z3,S3,...) combines, on the same axes, graphs defined for the quads *(Xi, Yi, Zi, Si)*. It is a way of representing various functions on the same graph.

Here is an example:

```
>> x = 0:pi/50:10*pi;
>> y = sin(x);
>> z = cos(x);
>> plot3(x, y, z)
```

This generates the graph in Figure 3-1.

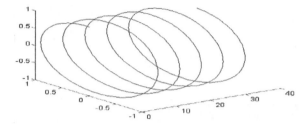

Figure 3-1.

3.2 Polygons in Three Dimensions

MATLAB also allows for drawing polygons in three dimensions. To do this, use the following commands:

fill3(X,Y,Z,C) draws the compact polygon whose vertices are the triples of the components *(Xi, Yi, Zi)* of the column vectors *X, Y* and *Z*. C can be a row vector of numbers, with the same number of columns as X and Y; or C can be a column vector of numbers, with the same number of rows as X and Y; or C can be a character that uses the colorspec characters shown like 'k' for black. When C is a numeric vector, it is used as a scaled index into the current colormap. If *X, Y* and *Z* are of the same dimension, several polygons corresponding to each triple vector column *(X.j, Y.j, Z.j)* may be represented as matrices simultaneously. In this case, *C* can be a row vector. *Cj* elements determine the unique color of each polygon corresponding to the triple of vector column *(X.j, Y.j, Z.j)*. C may also be an array of the same dimension as *X, Y* and *Z*, in which case the elements determine the colors of each point *(Xijk, Yijk, Zijk)* of the set of polygons.

fill3(X1,Y1,Z1,C1,X2,Y2, Z2, C2,...) draws the compact polygon whose vertices are given by the points *(Xi, Yi, Zi)* and Ci.

Here is an example:

```
>> x = cos(0:0.01:8*pi);
>> y = sin(0:0.01:8*pi);
>> z = 0:0.01:8*pi;
>> fill3(x,y,z,'r')
```

This generates the graph of Figure 3-2.

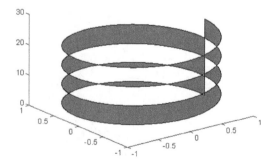

Figure 3-2.

3.3 Graphics in Parametric 3-D Coordinates

Let's see here how MATLAB draws curves in parametric coordinates in space, also known as **warped curves in parametric coordinates**. The fundamental problem is to get graphs of tridimensional functions in which *the variable x, y and z* depend, in turn, on a parameter *t*.

The command that can be used is **plot3** and all its variants, by suitably defining intervals of variation of the parameter, not by the independent variable as it was until now.

This type of graphic is very useful in certain matters, such as, for example, differential geometry.

Here is an example:

```
>> t = -4*pi:0.01:4*pi;
>> x = cos(t) .^ 2;
>> y = sin(t) .* cos (t);
>> z = sin(t);
>> plot3(x, y, z)
```

This generates the graph in Figure 3-3.

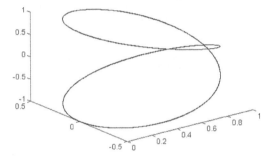

Figure 3-3.

3.4 Surfaces, Meshes and Contours

So far we have seen the 3D graphics based on a line that moves in three dimensions to form a warped curve. Now let's see how *3D graphics corresponding to surfaces and their different variants* are made available.

3.5 Surfaces in Explicit Coordinates

Surface graphics allow for dense representations of tridimensional figures, and in particular of functions of two variables. The first step in representing a function of two variables $z = f(x,y)$ using a surface chart, is to use the command *meshgrid*, which basically defines the array of points (X, Y) on which the function of two variables is evaluated for its graphical representation. Its syntax is as follows:

```
[X, Y] = meshgrid(x,y)
```

Parameters x and y are vectors that are replicated into to matrices X and Y. Each matrix will have the same number of rows as the length of x, and the same number of columns as the length of y. The increments of values in each of the vectors determine the "spacing" of the resulting grid. For example, x of [-10:0.1:10] and y of [-2:0.1:2] will result in X of 40 columns and 100 rows. Each columns will have the same sequence of values between -10 and +10. While Y will also have 40 columns and 100 rows, each of the rows will have the same sequence of values between -2 and +2.

The second step is to use the available commands to effect the result, which are as follows:

surf(X,Y,Z,C) represents the graph of the function's surface $z = f(x,y)$, using the colors specified in C. The C argument can be ignored.

surfc(X,Y,Z,C) represents the graph of the function's surface $z = f(x,y)$ with the chart's corresponding isolines (contour lines projected onto the XY-plane).

surfl(X, Y, Z) represents the graph of the function's surface $z = f(x,y)$, making the drawing with shading (highlights from a light source).

EXERCISE 3-1

Represent the surface of the slope-intercept form:

$$z = \frac{Sin\left(\sqrt{x^2 + y^2}\right)}{\sqrt{x^2 + y^2}} \quad -14/2 < \text{x, y} < 14/2$$

Also represent the surface with its contour.

```
>> [X, Y] = meshgrid(-7.5:.5:7.5);
>> Z = sin(sqrt(X.^2+Y.^2))./sqrt(X.^2+Y.^2);
>> surf(X, Y, Z)
```

This gives the graph of Figure 3-4.

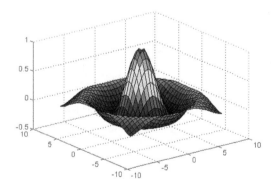

Figure 3-4.

The surface with the outline (contour) graph is shown in Figure 3-5. The following syntax is used:

```
>> [X, Y] = meshgrid(-7.5:.5:7.5);
>> Z = sin(sqrt(X.^2+Y.^2))./sqrt(X.^2+Y.^2);
>> surfc(X, Y, Z)
```

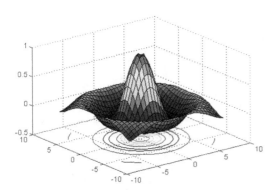

Figure 3-5.

Figure 3-6 shows the chart shaded, using the syntax:

```
>> [X, Y] = meshgrid(-7.5:.5:7.5);
>> Z = sin(sqrt(X.^2+Y.^2))./sqrt(X.^2+Y.^2);
>> surfl(X, Y, Z)
```

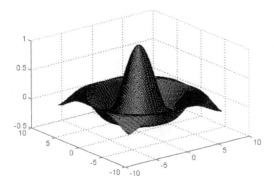

Figure 3-6.

3.6 Mesh Graphics

A three-dimensional mesh graph is defined by a function $z = f(x,y)$, so that the points on the surface are represented on a grid, result of the z values are given by $f(x,y)$ on corresponding points of the (x, y) plane. The appearance of a mesh chart is like a fishing net, with points on the surface on the nodes of the network. Actually, it is a graph of surface whose graph has the form of a network.

To represent a mesh graph, use the command ***mesh*** and its variants, whose syntax are as follows:

mesh(X,Y,Z,C) represents the graph of the mesh function $z = f(x,y)$, drawing the grid lines that compose the mesh with the colors specified in C. The C argument is optional.

meshz(X,Y,Z,C) represents the graph of the mesh function $z = f(x,y)$ with a curtain around the perimeter of the grid that drops to the bottom of the z-axis giving the impression of a draped tablecloth.

meshc(X,Y,Z,C) represents the graph of the mesh function $z = f(x,y)$ along with a corresponding contour chart like surfc above (with contour lines projected onto the XY-plane).

EXERCISE 3-2

Represent the mesh graph for the surface of equation:

$$z = xe^{(-x^2 - y^2)} \qquad -2 < x, y < 2$$

Also add their contours (a contour chart) and include a curtain.

The syntax presented here gives as a result the graph in Figure 3-7:

```
>> [X, Y] = meshgrid(-2:.1:2,-2:.1:2);
>> Z = X .* exp(-X.^2 - Y.^2);
>> mesh(X, Y, Z)
```

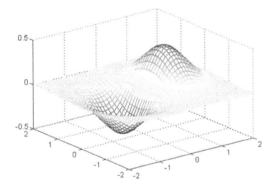

Figure 3-7.

Figure 3-8 presents the mesh along with the contour graph (or contour chart) for the syntax as follows:

```
>> [X, Y] = meshgrid(-2:.1:2,-2:.1:2);
>> Z = X .* exp(-X.^2 - Y.^2);
>> meshc(X, Y, Z)
```

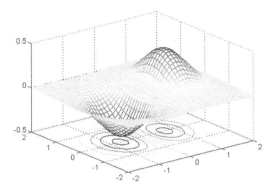

Figure 3-8.

Finally, Figure 3-9 represent the mesh graphic and curtain option. The syntax is as follows:

```
>> [X, Y] = meshgrid(-2:.1:2,-2:.1:2);
>> Z = X .* exp(-X.^2 - Y.^2);
>> meshz(X, Y, Z)
```

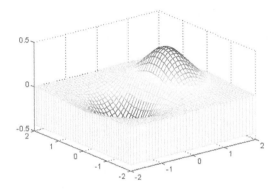

Figure 3-9.

3.7 Contour Graphics

Another option for visualizing a function of two variables is to use level curves calls (a system of dimensional planes. These curves are characterized as such because they are the points (x, y) on which the value of $f(x,y)$ is constant. Thus, for example, in the weather charts, level curves representing the same temperature points are called isotherms, and contour lines of equal pressure, isobars. Contour lines, representing heights (values of $f(x,y)$ that are equivalent, can describe surfaces in space. Thus, drawing different contours corresponding to constant heights, can be described as a map of lines on the surface level, MATLAB calls a *contour graph*. The contour plots can be represented in two and three dimensions.

A map showing the regions of the Earth's surface, whose contour lines represent the height above the sea level, is called a topographic map. These maps, therefore show the variance of $z = f(x,y)$ with respect to x and y. When the space between contour lines is large, it means that the variation of the variable z is slow, while a small space indicates a rapid change of z.

Commands used in MATLAB for the representation of isographs (contour lines) are as follows:

contour(Z) draws the outline graph (contour lines) for the Z matrix graph. The number of contour lines to be used are chosen automatically.

contour(Z,n) draws the graph outline (contour lines) for the Z matrix using n contour lines.

contour(x, y, Z, n) draws the graph outline (contour lines) for the Z matrix in the X and Y axes using scaling defined by the vectors x and y (with n contour lines).

contour3(Z), **contour3(Z,n)** and **contour3(x, y, Z, n)** draws the contour in 3-dimensional plots.

pcolor(X, Y, Z) draws a graph outline (contour lines) to the matrix (X, Y, Z) using a representation based on densities of colors. It is often called a density chart.

EXERCISE 3-3

Given the surface of equation:

$$z = \text{Sine}(x)\,\text{Sine}(y) \qquad -2 < x, y < 2$$

Represent it with its contour. Then represent its two-dimensional outline with 20 graph lines and its three-dimensional outline with 50 chart lines. Also draw the corresponding density chart.

Figure 3-10 shows the graph of the surface with its contour. The syntax is as follows:

```
>> [X, Y] = meshgrid(-2:0.1:2);
>> Z = sin(X) .* sin(Y);
>> surfc(X, Y, Z)
```

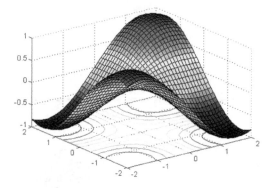

Figure 3-10.

Figure 3-11 shows the two-dimensional contour graph using 20 lines. The syntax is as follows:

```
>> [X, Y] = meshgrid(-2:0.1:2);
>> Z = sin(X) .* sin(Y);
>> contour(Z, 20)
```

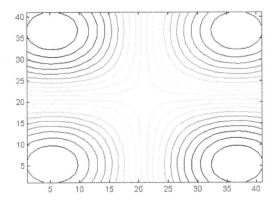

Figure 3-11.

Figure 3-12 shows the three-dimensional contour graph using 50 lines. The syntax is as follows:

```
>> [X, Y] = meshgrid(-2:0.1:2);
>> Z = sin(X) .* sin(Y);
>> contour3(Z, 50)
```

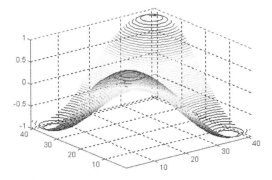

Figure 3-12.

Finally, Figure 3-13 represents the density graph (with the contour shaded according to different intensities of color). The syntax is as follows:

```
>> [X, Y] = meshgrid(-2:0.1:2);
>> Z = sin (X) .* sin(Y);
>> pcolor(X, Y, Z)
```

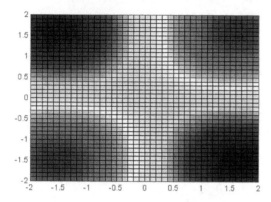

Figure 3-13.

3.8 Manipulating Three-Dimensional Graphics

There are commands in MATLAB which allow you to change the appearance of the same graph, either by your shader, the scale of its themes, colors, hidden lines, the point of view from which one can observe it, etc. Below, some of these commands are:

axis([xmin ymin, ymax, zmin zmax max *x*]) places intervals of variation of the axes at the indicated values. It lso accepts the options *'ij'*, *'square'*, *'equal'*, etc, identical to those already seen for two dimensions.

view([x, y, z]) places the point of view of the figure at the point's Cartesian coordinates *(x, y, z)*.

view([az, el]) puts the angle of view of the figure in the point of azimuth (horizontal rotation) *'az'* and elevation (vertical lift).

hidden controls the presence of hidden lines in the graph. These lines come with *hidden on* and go with *hidden off.*

shading controls the type of shadow of a surface created with commands *surf, mesh, pcolor, fill* and *fill3*. The option *shading flat* situates a smooth shading option. The option *shading interp* implements dense shading and the option *shading faceted* (the default) opts for normal shading.

colormap(M) locates the matrix *M* as the current color map. *M* must have three columns and only contain values between 0 and 1. It can also be a matrix whose rows are vectors RGB type *[r g b]*. All arrays must have 3 columns and *p* rows.

Brighten(p) adjusts the lighting of the figure. The variation of *p* is the interval *(-1,1)*, and as the values of *p* approach - *1*, the figure darkens, while as *p* values approach *1*, the figure illuminates.

image(A) produces a two-dimensional image with colors based upon the values of the elements of the array A, and is used to display photographs and drawings adapted to the specified colormap. Each element *(m, n)* of the matrix *A* affects a rectangular section of the image.

caxis([cmin cmax]) places the minimum and maximum values of the color scale (defined by the colormap and intrinsically related to the divisions that are made in the axes via grids) for a chart. Therefore, it enables you to use only a subset of colors defined by the colormap.

EXERCISE 3-4

Given the surface equation:

$$z = x^2 - y^2 \qquad -2 < x, y < 2$$

represent it with strong lighting, dense shadows and gray colors. Using the same axis, show four different points of view and with the shading by default.

```
>> [X, Y] = meshgrid(-2:0.05:2);
>> surf(X,Y,Z),shading interp,brighten(0.75),colormap(gray(5))
```

This generates the graph in Figure 3-14.

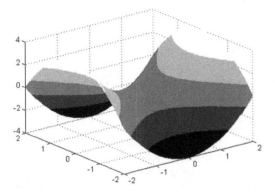

Figure 3-14.

We will now present in Figure 3-15 the surface focused from four different points of view. The syntax is as follows:

```
>> [X, Y] = meshgrid(-2:0.05:2);
>> Z = X .^ 2 - Y .^ 2;
>> subplot(2,2,1)
>> surf(X,Y,Z)
>> subplot(2,2,2)
>> surf(X,Y,Z),view(-90,0)
>> subplot(2,2,3)
>> surf(X,Y,Z),view(60,30)
>> subplot(2,2,4)
>> surf (X, Y, Z), view (- 10, 30)
```

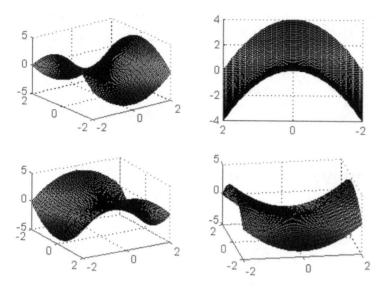

Figure 3-15.

3.9 Parametric Surfaces

MATLAB allows you to represent surfaces whose components depend on specified variations in parameters. To do this, you can use the commands *surf* and *mesh*, by properly defining *the variables x, and z.*

Cylindrical and spherical coordinate surfaces are representable in MATLAB, parameterizing them in advance.

In terms of surfaces of revolution, they always require ranges, which allow their graphical representation with MATLAB.

EXERCISE 3-5

Draw the surface of parametric coordinates:

$$x = 4\cos(r)\sec(t) \quad y = 2\text{sine}(r)\sec(t) \quad z = \tan(t) \quad -2\pi < r < 2\pi, \ -\pi < r < \pi$$

```
>> r = [-2*pi:0.1:2*pi]';
>> t = [-pi:0.1:pi];
>> X = 4 * cos(r) * sec(t);
>> Y = 2 * sin(r) * sec(t);
>> Z = ones(size(r)) * tan(t);
>> surf(X,Y,Z)
>> shading interp
```

Note that "ones" as used above is a function that produces a vector or matrix that is populated by ones. Similarly, "zeros" is populated by zeroes.

The graph is shown in Figure 3-16.

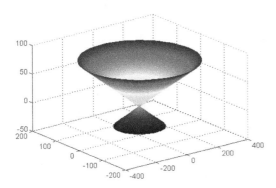

Figure 3-16.

EXERCISE 3-6

Create the graph of the surface of revolution that is turning the function Sine (x) around the Z axis. also create the graph of the surface of revolution rotating the function e ^ x around the Y axis.

To obtain the equation of the surface, on the assumption that the rotation is around the Z axis, consider the graph of the generating curve $y = r(z)$ in the plane YZ. Turning this graph around the Z axis forms a surface of revolution. The sections with flat $z = z0$ are circles whose RADIUS is $r(z_0)$ and equation $x^2 + y^2 = [r(z_0)]^2$. That means that the equation $x^2 + y^2 = [r(z)]^2$ describes the points on the surface of revolution. For our problem, we have $r(z) = Sine(z)$ and the curve $x^2 + y^2 = Sine[z]^2$, which are parametric for the purpose of input for MATLAB graphics:

```
>> r =(0:0.1:2*pi)';
>> t =(-pi:0.1:2*pi);
>> X= cos (r)*sin (t);
>> Y= sin(r)*sin (t);
>> Z= ones (1, size (r))'* t;
>> surf(X,Y,Z), shading interp
```

This generates the graph in Figure 3-17.

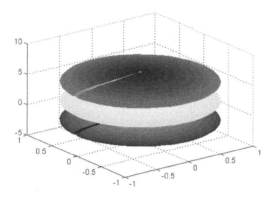

Figure 3-17.

If we propose this MATLAB entry:

```
r =(0:0.1:2*pi)';
t =(-2:0.1:2);
X= cos (r)*exp (t);
Y= ones(1, size(r))'*t;
Z= sin(r)*exp (t);
surf(X,Y,Z), shading interp
```

You get the graph in Figure 3-18, which has been found in the same way as the previous one, but rotating the exponential function around the Y axis (the generating curve is now the function $e \wedge x$).

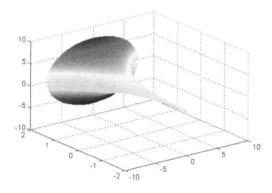

Figure 3-18.

EXERCISE 3-7

Represent the cylinder {t, Sine [t], u}, with {t, 0, 2Pi} and {u, 0, 4} by revolving {Cos [t](3+Cos[u]), Sine [t]
(3+Cos[u]), Sine [u]}, with {t, 0, 2 Pi} and {u, 0, 2Pi}.

```
>> t = [0:0.1:2*pi]';
>> r = [0:0.1:4];
>> X = sin(t) * ones(size(r));
>> Y = cos(t) * ones(size(r));
>> Z = ones(size(t)) * r;
>> surf(X,Y,Z)
>> shading interp
```

You get the graph in Figure 3-19.

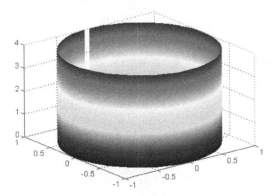

Figure 3-19.

To represent the torus of revolution, we use the following syntax:

```
>> r = [0:0.1:2*pi]';
>> t = [0:0.1:2*pi];
>> X = [3 + cos(r)] * cos(t);
>> Y = [3 + cos(r)] * sin(t);
>> Z = sin(t)' * ones(size(t));
>> surf(X,Y,Z)
>> shading interp
```

We get the graph in Figure 3-20.

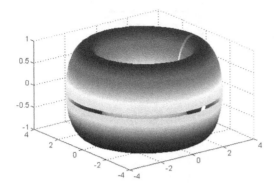

Figure 3-20.

3.10 Special Geometric Forms

MATLAB enables commands to generate cylinders and spheres. We have:

> **[X, Y, Z] = cylinder(r, n)** draws the cylinder generated by the curve *r*, which has *n* points (*n = 20* per default) on the horizontal section of the circumference that is aligned with the *Z* axis.

> **[X, Y, Z] = sphere (n)** draws a sphere (by default *n = 20*).

As an example, let's represent the cylinder generated by the curve *4Cos (t)* when *t* varies between *0* and *2π*. The syntax will be as follows:

```
>> t = 0:pi/10:2 * pi;
>> [X, Y, Z] = cylinder(4 * cos(t));
>> surf(X, Y, Z)
```

This generates the graph of Figure 3-21.

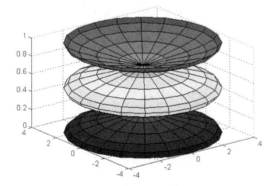

Figure 3-21.

3.11 Other Graphics Handling Options

Graphic characteristics treated so far belong to the high level MATLAB GUI. However, there are low level (**Handle Graphics**) commands that allow creation and manipulation of figures, axes, lines, surfaces, images, text, menus and other graphics objects. Some of the commands to create graphical objects are:

> **Figure(h)** or **h = figure** create the figure as an object of name *h*, and is located as a current figure. The **gcf(h)** *(get current handle)* command generally means return the handle to the figure. The command *close(h)* closes figure **h.** The command **whitebg(h)** changes the color of the background of the figure *h*. The command **clf** closes the current figure. The command **graymon** is used for legibility of grayscale. The command **refresh** redraws the figure.

> **axes(e)** or **e = axes** creates the axes as an object of name e, in the current figure. Use the command *gca(e)* to refer to any property of the e axes. *The **cla** command is used to delete all the objects referring to the current axes.*

> **l = line(x,y)** or **l = line(x, y, z)** creates an object of name *l*, the line joining the points *(X, Y)* in the flat, or *(X, Y, Z)* space.

> **p = patch(X, Y, C)** or **patch(X,Y,Z,C)** creates an opaque polygonal area that is defined by the set of points *(X, Y)* in the flat, or *(X, Y, Z)* space, and whose color is given by *C*, as an object of name *p*.

> **s = surface(X,Y,Z,C)** creates the parametric surface defined by *X*, *Y* and *Z* , and whose color is given by *C*, as an object of named *s*.

> **i = image(C)** creates the image defined by the colors in the array *C* as an object of name *i*.

> **t = text(x, y, 'string')** or **t = text(x, y, z, 'string')** creates the text defined by the parameter in single quotes, located at the point in the *(x, y)* plane, or at the point in the *(x, y, z)* space.

Each object has a level of hierarchy. The parents of an object are superior in the hierarchy, and children are the objects of a lower hierarchy. The object is created with *figure*, then, the one created by *axes* and, finally, and at the same level, are the ones created by *image*, *patch*, *surface*, *text* and *line*. This means that if, for example, you want to create a surface, first has to create the figure that is going to be graphed, then the axes, and, finally, the surface itself.

So far we have seen commands that allow you to create objects, but, in addition, all these objects can have properties, as style of line, color, etc. The list of possible properties for each object is very long, and so full knowledge of the list requires consultation of *MATLAB Reference* manual, http://www.mathworks.com/help/matlab/. As a general rule, the name of a property of an object is a compound word whose components begin with capital letter. For example, the line style property has the name *LineStyle*. The names of the properties that are mapped by default to an object start with *Default*, as, for example, *DefaultFigureColor*, which assigns the color by default to a figure. Below, are some of the most typical properties for the different objects.

Object	Properties	Possible values
Figure	*Color (background color)*	*'y', 'c', 'r', 'g', 'b', 'w', 'k'*
	ColorMap	*hot(p), gray(p), pink(p),....*
	Position	*[left, bottom, width, height]*
	Name	*string name*
	MinColorMap (min. color no.)	*minimum number of colors for map*
	NextPlot (graph mode.)	*new, add, replace*
	NumberTitle (No. in the figure)	*on, off*
	Units (units of measurement)	*pixels, inches, centimeters, points*
	Resize (size figure with mouse)	*on (can be changed), off (no)*
Axes	*Box (box for the chart)*	*on, off*
	Color (color of the axes)	*'y', 'c', 'r', 'g', 'b', 'w', 'k'*
	GridLineStyle (line for mesh)	*'-', '--', ':', '-.'*
	Position	*[left, bottom, width, height]*
	TickLength (length between marks)	*a numeric value*
	TickDir (direction of)	*in, out*
	Units	*pixels, inches, centimeters, points*
	View (view)	*[azimuth, elevation]*
	FontAngle (angle of source)	*normal, italic, oblique*
	FontName (name of source)	*the name of the source font*
	FontSize (font size)	*numeric value*
	FontWeight (weight)	*light, normal, demi, bold*
	DrawMode (drawing mode)	*normal, fast*
	XDir, YDir, ZDir (direction of axes)	*normal (growing from left to right), reverse*
	XGrid, YGrid, ZGrid (grids)	*on, off*
	XLabel, YLabel, Zlabel (tags)	*string containing the text of labels*
	XLim, YLim, ZLim (limit values)	*[min, max] (range of variation)*
	XScale, YScale, ZScale (scales)	*linear, log (log)*
	XTick,YTick,ZTick	*[m1,m2,...] (situation marks on axis)*
Line	*Color (color of the line)*	*'y', 'c', 'r', 'g', 'b', 'w', 'k'*
	LineStyle (line style)	*'-', '--', ':', '-.', '+', '*', '.', 'x'*
	LineWidth (line width)	*numeric value*
	Visible (visible line or not displayed.)	*on, off*
	XData, YData, ZData (coordinates)	*set of coordinates of the line*

(continued)

Object	Properties	Possible values
Text	Color (text color)	'y', ' 'c', 'r', 'g', 'b', 'w', 'k'
	FontAngle (angle of source)	normal, italic, oblique
	FontName (name of source)	the name of the source font
	FontSize (font size)	numeric value
	FontWeight (weight)	light, normal, demi, bold
	HorizontalAlignment (hor setting.)	left, center, right
	VerticalAlignment (adjust to vert.)	top, cap, middle, baseline, bottom
	Position (position on screen)	[x, y, z] (point of situation)
	Rotation (orientation of the text)	0, ±90, ±180, ±270
	Units (units of measurement)	pixels, inches, centimeters, points
	String	the text string
Surface	CData (color of each point)	color matrix
	EdgeColor (color grids)	'y','m',..., none, flat, interp
	FaceColor (color of the faces)	'y','m',..., none, flat, interp
	LineStyle (line style)	'-', '--', ':', '-.', '+', '*', '.', 'x'
	LineWidth (line width)	numeric value
	MeshStyle (lines in rows and col.)	row, column, both
	Visible (visible line or not displayed.)	on, off
	XData, YData, ZData (coordinates)	set of coordinates of the surface
Patch	CData (color of each point)	color matrix
	EdgeColor (color of the axes)	'y', 'm',..., none, flat, interp
	FaceColor (color of the faces)	'y','m',..., none, flat, interp
	LineWidth (line width)	numeric value
	Visible (visible line or not displayed)	on, off
	XData, YData, ZData (coordinates)	set of coordinates of the surface
Image	CData (color of each point)	color matrix
	XData, YData (coordinates)	set of coordinates of the image

Among the commands that allow you to perform operations with graphical objects already created are as follows:

set(h, 'propertyname, 'propertyvalue',...) sets the specified properties to the provided values for the object *h*.

get(h, 'property') returns the current value of the specified property of the object *h*.

object = gco returns the current object of the current figure.

rotate(h, [a, e], α, [p,q,r]) rotates the object *h* by the angle α, according to the axis of azimuth, *elevation and the origin point (p, q, r)* (which is optional, and is the origin point of the axis of rotation, which is the center of the plot if not provided).

reset(h) updates all properties assigned to the object *h* and set its properties to their defaults.

delete(h) deletes the object *h*.

Here are some examples:
The following syntax changes the limits of variation of the current *X, Y* and *Z* axes to the specified values:

```
>> set(gca, 'XLim', [0,10], 'YLim', [-25, 25], 'ZLim', [-8,10])
```

The following syntax places the color of the background of the current figure in white:

```
>> set(gcf, 'Color', 'w')
```

The following syntax returns the current properties for the surface previously created and assigned to the variable named *surfh*:

```
>> get(surfh)
```

The following syntax returns the line style to that of the surface *surfh:*

```
>> get(surfh, 'LineStyle')
```

The following syntax deletes the surface *surfh*:

```
>> delete(surfh)
```

EXERCISE 3-8

Represent coordinates of the following parametric surface:

$$x(t) = 4\cos(r)\cos(t), \ y(t) = 2\text{sine}(r)\cos(t), \ z(t) = \text{sine}(t) \quad -\pi < r < \pi, \ -\pi/2 < t < \pi/2$$

so that it is presented in a figure with title "Parametric Surface" and whose background color is white, with a black colored axis with the surface itself presented in a grid, colored according to the jet colormap, and enclosed in a cube.

```
>> r = [-pi:0.1:pi]';
t = [-pi/2:0.1:pi/2];
x = 4*cos(r)*cos(t);
y = 2*sin(r)*cos(t);
z = ones(1,size(r))'*sin(t);
surface = surf(x, y, z);
set(surface,'EdgeColor', interp')
set(gcf, 'Color', 'w', 'Name', 'Parametric Surface');
set(gca,'XColor', 'k', 'YColor', 'k', 'ZColor', 'k', 'Box', 'on');
```

Figure 3-22 represents the ordered surface.

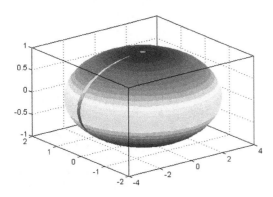

Figure 3-22.

CHAPTER 4

■ ■ ■

Display Volumes and Specialized Graphics

4.1 Volumes Visualization

MATLAB has a group of commands that allow you to represent different types of volumes. The following is the syntax of the most important.

---

coneplot(X, Y, Z, U, V, W, Cx, Cy, Cz)
coneplot(U, V, W, Cx, Cy, Cz)
coneplot(...,s)
coneplot(...,color)
coneplot(...,'quiver')
coneplot(...,'method')
coneplot(X, Y, Z, U, V, W, 'nointerp')
h = coneplot(...)

Vector graphics cones in 3-D vector fields. (X, Y, Z) define the coordinates of the vector field. (U, V, W) define the vector field. (Cx, Cy, Cz) define the location of the cones in the vector field. In addition they may include arguments such as color, method of interpolation, etc.

contourslice(X, Y, Z, V, Sx, Sy, Sz)
contourslice(X, Y, Z, V, Xi, Yi, Zi)
contourslice(V, Sx, Sy, Sz), contourslice (V, Xi, Yi, Zi)
contourslice(...,n)
contourslice(..., cvals)
contourslice(..., [cv cv])
contourslice(...,'method')
h = contourslice (...)

Draws outlines in planar sections of volumes according to the vectors (Sx, Sy, Sz). X, Y, Z define the coordinates for the volume V. Xi, Yi, Zi defined the surface along which the contour is drawn. You can use a method of interpolation and a number n of contour lines by plane. The value cv indicates a single-plane contour.

[curlx, curly, curlz, cav] = curl(X,Y,Z,U,V,W)
[curlx, curly, curlz, cav] = curl(U,V,W)
[curlz, cav] = curl(X,Y,U,V)
[curlz, cav] = curl(U,V)
[curlx,curly,curlz] = curl(...),
[curlx,curly] = curl(...)
cav = curl(...)

This concerns the rotational curl and the angular velocity vector field cav. (X, Y, Z) arrays define the coordinates for the(U, V, W) vector field. In the case of curl(U,V,W) the conditions have to be [X Y Z] = meshgrid (1:n, 1:m, 1:p) with [m, n, p] = size(V)

div = divergence(X,Y,Z,U,V,W)
div = divergence(U,V,W)
div = divergence(X,Y,U,V)
div = divergence(U,V)

The divergence of a vector field

(continued)

interpstreamspeed(X,Y,Z,U,V,W,vertices) **interpstreamspeed(U,V,W,vertices)** **interpstreamspeed(X,Y,Z,speed,vertices)** **interpstreamspeed(speed,vertices)** **interpstreamspeed(X,Y,U,V,vertices)** **interpstreamspeed(U,V,vertices)** **interpstreamspeed(X,Y,speed,vertices)** **interpstreamspeed(speed,vertices)** **interpstreamspeed(...,sf)** **vertsout = interpstreamspeed (...)**	*Interpolates streamline vertices based on the speed of the vector data.*
fvc = isocaps(X,Y,Z,V,isovalor) **fvc = isocaps(V, isovalue)** **fvc = isocaps(...,'enclose')** **fvc = isocaps(...,'whichplane')** **[f, v, (c)] = isocaps(...)** **isocaps(...)**	*Concerns isosurfaces of volume V in the form value. X, Y, Z are the coordinates of the volume V. If it is not given, (X, Y, Z) is supposed to be [X, Y, Z] = meshgrid (1: n, 1:m, 1:p) with [m, n, p] = size (V). The value enclose may be 'above' or 'below', specifying whether the end-caps enclose data values above or below the value specified in isovalue. The values that can be provided for the whichplane parameter indicate the plane of drawing (all, xmin, xmax, ymin, ymax, zmin, and zmax).*
CN = isocolors(X,Y,Z,C,vertices) **CN = isocolors(X,Y,Z,R,G,B,vertices)** **NC = isocolors (C, vertices)** **NC = isocolors (R, G, B, vertices)** **nc = isocolors(...,PatchHandle)** **isocolors(...,PatchHandle)**	*Computes the colors of the vertices of the isosurfaces using colors given as C or RGB values. PatchHandle vertices can be used.*
n = isonormals(X,Y,Z,V,vertices) **n = isonormals(V, vertices)** **n = isonormals(V, p),** **n = isonormals(X,Y,Z,V,p)** **n = isonormals(...,'negate')** **isonormals(V, p), isonormals(X,Y,Z,V,p)**	*Computes normal vertices of isosurfaces. The negate option changes the direction of the normals and p is a vertex object identifier. If the n argument is not listed, the isonormals are drawn.*
FV = isosurface(X,Y,Z,V,isovalue) **fv = isosurface(V, isovalue)** **FV = isosurface(X, Y, Z, V),** **FV = isosurface(X, Y, Z, V)** **fvc = isosurface(...,colors)** **fv = isosurface(...,'noshare')** **fv = isosurface(...,'verbose')** **[f, v] = isosurface(...)** **isosurface(...)**	*Extract data concerning the isosurfaces of volume V at the value specified in isovalue. The noshare argument indicates shared vertices will not be created and progress messages are printed to the command window as the function progresses through its computations.*
reducepatch(p,r) **nfv = reducepatch(p,r)** **nfv = reducepatch(fv,r)** **reducepatch(...,'fast')** **reducepatch(...,'verbose')** **nfv = reducepatch(f,v,r)** **[NC, nv] = reducepatch (...)**	*It reduces the number of faces of the object identified by p with a factor of reduction r. The argument fast indicates that shared vertices are not computed, while NC and nv indicates that faces and vertices are returned. reducepatch(p) and NFV=reducepatch(FV) use a reduction factor of 0.5.*

(continued)

[nx, ny, nz, nv] = reducevolume(X,Y,Z,V,[Rx,Ry,Rz]) [nx, ny, nz, nv] = reducevolume(V,[Rx,Ry,Rz]) nv = reducevolume(...)	*Reduces the number of items in the data set of volume V whose coordinates are (X, Y, Z) arrays. Every Rx element is kept in the x direction, every Ry element is kept in the y direction, and every Rz element is kept in the z direction. For example, if Rx is 4, every fourth value in the x direction from the original dataset is retained.*
shrinkfaces(p,sf) nfv = shrinkfaces(p,sf) nfv = shrinkfaces(fv,sf) shrinkfaces(p), shrinkfaces(fv) nfv = shrinkfaces(f,v,sf) [nf,nv] = shrinkfaces(...)	*Collapses the size of the faces of the object identified by p according to a contraction sf factor. If fv and sf are passed, the faces and vertices in fv are used.*
W = smooth3(V) W = smooth3(V,'filter') W = smooth3(V,'filter',size) W = smooth3(V,'filter',size,sd)	*Smooths data of volume V. Smoothing with Gaussian or box filters.You can use a scalar or triple for anti-aliasing (size) and a standard deviation (sd); this only applies when 'gaussian' filter mode is used.*
XY = stream2(x,y,u,v,startx,starty) XY = stream2(u,v,startx,starty)	*Finds lines of the current 2D vector data (u, v) whose coordinates are defined by the arrays (x, y)*
XYZ = stream3(X,Y,Z,U,V,W,startx,starty,startz) XYZ = stream3(U,V,W,startx,starty,startz)	*Finds lines of the current 3D data vector (u, v, w) whose coordinates are defined by the arrays (x, y, z)*
h = streamline(X,Y,Z,U,V,W,startx,starty,startz) h = streamline(U,V,W,startx,starty,startz) h = streamline(XYZ) h = streamline(X,Y,U,V,startx,starty) h = streamline(U,V,startx,starty) h = streamline(XY)	*Draw lines of the current 2D or 3D data vector. (X, Y, Z) are the coordinates of (U, V, W) and (startx, starty, startz) indicate the starting positions of the lines.*
streamparticles(vertices) streamparticles(vertices, n)	*Draws the vector of the data field particles and represents them by markers in 2D or 3D vertices.*
streamribbon(X,Y,Z,U,V,W,startx,starty,startz) streamribbon(U,V,W,startx,starty,startz) streamribbon(vertices,X,Y,Z,cav,speed) streamribbon(vertices,cav,speed) streamribbon(vertices,twistangle) streamribbon(...,width), h = streamribbon(...)	*Draws tapes for vector volume data (U, V, W) whose coordinates are (X, Y, Z) arrays using(startx, starty, startz) to indicate the positions of the start of the tapes.*
streamslice(X,Y,Z,U,V,W,startx,starty,startz) streamslice(U,V,W,startx,starty,startz) streamslice(X,Y,U,V) streamslice(U,V) streamslice(...,density) streamslice(...,'arrowmode') streamslice(...,'method') h = streamslice(...) [vertices arrowvertices] = streamslice(...)	*Draws stream lines well spaced with arrow keys for the vector volume data (U, V, W) whose coordinates are (X, Y, Z), arrays where (startx, starty, startz) indicate the start positions of the lines. Density is a positive number that modifies the spacing of lines, arrows mode can use the values arrows or noarrows to put or not at the ends in the arrows, and method indicates the type of interpolation (linear, cubic, or nearest).*

(continued)

streamtube(X,Y,Z,U,V,W,startx,starty,startz) **streamtube(U,V,W,startx,starty,startz)** **streamtube(vertices,X,Y,Z,divergence)** **streamtube(vertices, divergence)** **streamtube(vertices,width)** **streamtube(vertices)** **streamtube(…,[scale n])** **h = streamtube(…)**	*Draws tubes from vector volume data (U, V, W) whose coordinates are (X, Y, Z) arrays; (startx, starty, startz) indicate the start positions of the tubes. If the parameters vertices and divergence are used, then it is expected that [X Y Z] of vertices are sized as meshgrid(1:n, 1:m, 1:p) where [M N P] = size(divergence); width indicates the width of the tubes (which may be affected by a scale parameter n)*
fvc = surf2patch(h) **fvc = surf2patch(Z)** **fvc = surf2patch(Z,C)** **fvc = surf2patch(X,Y,Z)** **fvc = surf2patch(X, Y, Z, C)** **fvc = surf2patch(…,'triangles')** **[f,v,c] = surf2patch(…)**	*Converts a given surface returning faces, vertices and color structure into the patch formatted structure fvc. The object can be given even as a surface in its different forms. You can also create triangular faces using the triangles argument.*
[Nx, Ny, Nz, Nv] = subvolume(X,Y,Z,V,limits) **[Nx, Ny, Nz, Nv] = subvolume(V,limits)** **Nv = subvolume (…)**	*Extracts a subset of the volume V (X, Y, Z) using the given limits (limits = [xmin, xmax, ymin, ymax, zmin, zmax])*
lims = volumebounds(X,Y,Z,V) **lims = volumebounds(X,Y,Z,U,V,W)** **lims = volumebounds(V)** **lims = volumebounds(U,V,W)**	*Gives coordinates and boundaries of colors for the volume V (U, V, W) whose coordinates are (X, Y, Z) arrays.*
v = flow, v = flow(n) or v = flow(x,y,z)	*Generates fluid flow data that is useful in functions that present volume data. When the x, y, and z parameters are used, the speed profile is evaluated.*

A first example are vectors that depict speed using cones in a vector field (Figure 4-1) from the default MATLAB data set *wind.mat* using the code below:

```
>> load wind
xmin = min(x(:)); xmax = max(x(:)); ymin = min(y(:));
ymax = max(y (:)); zmin = min(z(:));
daspect([2 2 1])
xrange = linspace(xmin,xmax,8);
yrange = linspace(ymin,ymax,8);
zrange = 3:4:15;
[cx cy cz] = meshgrid(xrange, yrange, zrange);
hcones = coneplot(x,y,z,u,v,w,cx,cy,cz,5);
set(hcones,'FaceColor','red','EdgeColor','none')
```

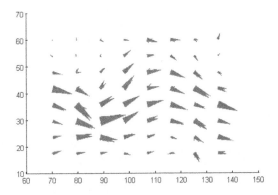

Figure 4-1.

We then create planes along the axes (Figure 4-2).

```
>> hold on
wind_speed = sqrt(u.^2 + v.^2 + w.^2);
hsurfaces = slice(x,y,z,wind_speed,[xmin,xmax],ymax,zmin);
set(hsurfaces,'FaceColor','interp','EdgeColor','none')
hold off
```

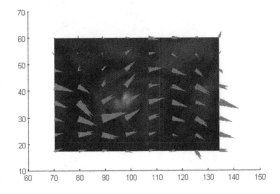

Figure 4-2.

Finally we define an appropriate point of view (Figure 4-3).

```
>> axis tight; view(30,40); axis off
```

Figure 4-3.

They are then drawn as contours in planar sections of volumes on the data set *wind.mat* with a suitable point of view (Figure 4-4).

```
>> [x y z v] = flow;
h = contourslice(x,y,z,v,[1:9],[],[0],linspace(-8,2,10));
axis([0,10,-3,3,-3,3]); daspect([1,1,1])
set(gcf,'Color',[.5,.5,.5],'Renderer','zbuffer')
```

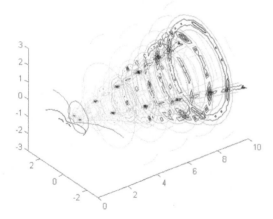

Figure 4-4.

The following example shows the rotational vector field given by *wind.mat* using sections with colored drawings (Figure 4-5).

```
>> load wind
cav = curl(x,y,z,u,v,w);
slice(x,y,z,cav,[90 134],[59],[0]);
shading interp
daspect([1 1 1]); axis tight
colormap hot(16)
camlight
```

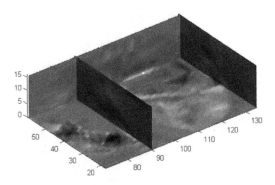

Figure 4-5.

■ **Note**   camlight adds a light, just like a camera shoot. camlight with no parameters is the same as camlight right, which places the light above and to the right of the camera. Without this, the image would be much more yellow and orange and the vertical surface on the left would be much harder to perceive.

Below is code to show a representation on a plane (Figure 4-6).

```
>> load wind
k = 4;
x = x(:,:,k); y = y(:,:,k); u = u(:,:,k); v = v(:,:,k);
cav = curl(x,y,u,v);
pcolor(x,y,cav); shading interp
hold on;
quiver(x,y,u,v,'y')
hold off
colormap copper
```

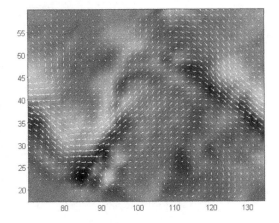

Figure 4-6.

The following example represents the divergence of the vector field given by *wind.mat* using sections with colored drawings (Figure 4-7).

```
>> load wind
div = divergence(x,y,z,u,v,w);
slice(x,y,z,div,[90 134],[59],[0]);
shading interp
daspect([1 1 1])
camlight
colormap jet
```

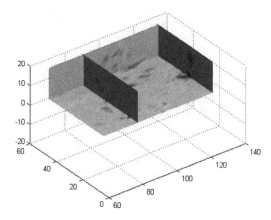

Figure 4-7.

Below is an example concerning colors and normal for a given isosurface (Figure 4-8).

```
>> [x y z] = meshgrid(1:20,1:20,1:20);
data = sqrt(x.^2 + y.^2 + z.^2);
cdata = smooth3(rand(size(data)),'box',7);
p = patch(isosurface(x,y,z,data,10));
isonormals(x, y, z, data, p);
isocolors(x, y, z, cdata, p);
set(p,'FaceColor','interp','EdgeColor','none')
view(150,30); daspect([1 1 1]);axis tight
camlight; lighting phong;
```

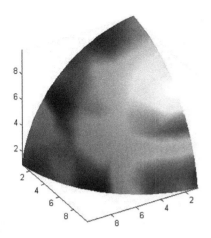

Figure 4-8.

Subsequently represented is an isosurface (Figure 4-9) based on the *wind.mat* data set.

```
>> [x, y, z, v] = flow;
p = patch(isosurface(x,y,z,v,-3));
isonormals(x,y,z,v,p)
set(p,'FaceColor','blue','EdgeColor','none');
daspect([1 1 1])
view(3); axis tight
```

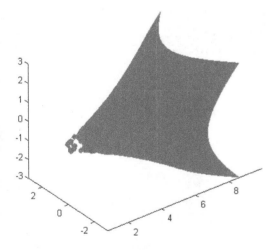

Figure 4-9.

81

In the following example (Figure 4-10), we reduce the faces of the anterior surface by 15% and show both images for comparison.

```
>> [x,y,z,v] = flow;
p = patch(isosurface(x,y,z,v,-3));
set(p,'facecolor','w','EdgeColor','b');
daspect([1,1,1])
view(3)
figure;
h = axes;
p2 = copyobj(p,h);
reducepatch(p2,0.15)
daspect([1,1,1])
view(3)
```

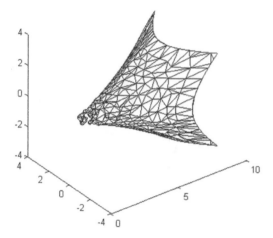

Figure 4-10.

The following example reduces the volume of the previous isosurface (Figure 4-11) and then shrinks the size of their faces (Figure 4-12).

```
>> [x, y, z, v] = flow;
[x, y, z, v] = reducevolume(x,y,z,v,2);
FV = isosurface(x,y,z,v,-3);
p1 = patch(FV);
set(p1,'FaceColor','red','EdgeColor',[.5,.5,.5]);
daspect([1 1 1]); view(3); axis tight
title('Original')

>> figure
p2 = patch(shrinkfaces(FV,.3));
set(p2,'FaceColor','red','EdgeColor',[.5,.5,.5]);
daspect([1 1 1]); view (3); axis tight
title ('after the contraction of faces')
```

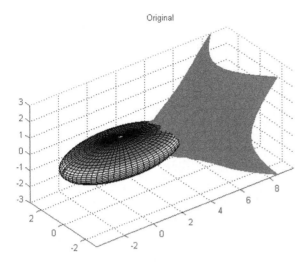

Figure 4-11.

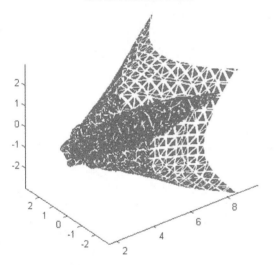

Figure 4-12.

The following creates a chart with lines of two dimensional current (Figure 4-13) and then for three-dimensional (Figure 4-14).

```
>> load wind
[sx,sy] = meshgrid(80,20:10:50);
streamline(stream2(x(:,:,5),y(:,:,5),u(:,:,5),v(:,:,5),sx,sy));

>> load wind
[sx sy sz] = meshgrid(80,20:10:50,0:5:15);
streamline(stream3(x,y,z,u,v,w,sx,sy,sz))
view(3)
```

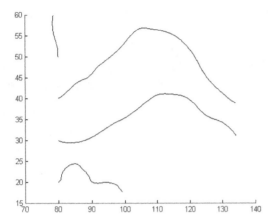

Figure 4-13.

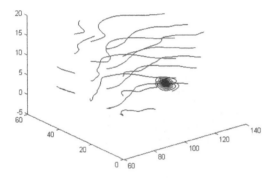

Figure 4-14.

Below is a chart of tape (Figure 4-15) and one of tube (Figure 4-16).

```
>> load wind
[sx sy sz] = meshgrid(80,20:10:50,0:5:15);
daspect([1 1 1])
verts = stream3(x,y,z,u,v,w,sx,sy,sz);
CAV = curlx,y,z,u,v,w);
spd = sqrt(u.^2 + v.^2 + w.^2).*.1;
streamribbon(verts,x,y,z,CAV,spd)

>> load wind
[sx sy sz] = meshgrid(80,20:10:50,0:5:15);
daspect([1 1 1])
streamtube(x,y,z,u,v,w,sx,sy,sz);
```

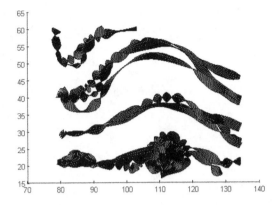

Figure 4-15.

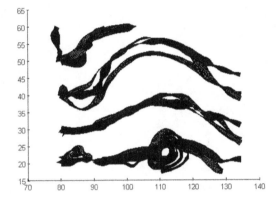

Figure 4-16.

4.2 Specialized Graphics

There are several types of specialized graphics that can be done with MATLAB (areas, boxes, graphics, three-dimensional sectors of Pareto, etc.) by using the commands that are presented in the following table.

area(Y)	*Makes the areas graph proportional to the values relative to the frequencies vector.*
area(X, Y)	*When X is provided it represents the values of the X axis, at which each corresponding Y value will be plotted.*
area(...,ymin)	*Specifies the lower limit in the Y axis direction of the fill area*
box on, box off	*Enable / disable boxes in axes for y in 3-D and 2-D graphics.*
comet(y)	*Makes the comet graphic relative to the vector of frequencies y*
comet(x, y)	*Performs the comet graphic relative to the frequencies vector Y whose elements are given by the vector X.*
comet(x, y, p)	*Comet graph with body of length p * length*

(continued)

ezcontour(f)	*Graphic of contour f(x,y) in [-2π, 2π] x [-2π, 2π]. So both the x and y parameters in the function are evaluated throughout the range of -2pi to +2pi.*
ezcontour(f, domain)	*Graphic of contour f(x,y) in the given domain*
ezcontour(...,n)	*Graphic of contour f(x,y) in mesh n x n*
ezcontourf(f)	*Graphic of contour f(x,y) filling in [-2π, 2π] x [-2π, 2π]. Both the x and y parameters in the function are evaluated throughout the range of -2pi to +2pi.*
ezcontourf(f, domain)	*Graphic of contour f(x,y) filling in the given domain*
ezcontourf(...,n)	*Graphic of contour f(x,y) stuffed in the mesh n x n*
ezmesh(f)	*Graph of f(x,y) mesh filling at [-2π, 2π] x [-2π, 2π]. Both the x and y parameters in the function are evaluated throughout the range of -2pi to +2pi.*
ezmesh(f,domain)	*Graphic mesh of f(x,y) filling in the given domain*
ezmesh(...,n)	*Graph of f(x,y) mesh padding in the mesh nxn*
ezmesh(x, y, z)	*Graphic mesh for x = x(t,u), y = y(t,u), z = z(t,u) t,u∈ [-2π, 2π]*
ezmesh(x, y, z, domain)	*Graphic mesh for x = x(t,u), y = y(t,u), z = z(t,u) t,u∈ domain*
ezmesh(..., 'circ')	*Graphic mesh on a disk centered in the domain*
ezmeshc(f)	*Performs a combination of mesh and contour graphs.*
ezmeshc(f, domain)	
ezmeshc(...,n)	
ezmeshc(x, y, z)	
ezmeshc(x, y, z, domain)	
ezmeshc(..., 'circ')	
ezsurf(f)	*Makes a colored surface chart*
ezsurf(f, domain)	
ezsurf(...,n)	
ezsurf(x, y, z)	
ezsurf (x, y, z, domain)	
ezsurf(..., 'circ')	
ezsurfc(f)	*Performs a combination of surface and contour graphs*
ezsurfc(f, domain)	
ezsurfc(...,n)	
ezsurfc(x, y, z)	
ezsurfc (x, and z, domain)	
ezsurfc(..., 'circ')	
ezplot3(x, y, z)	*Parametric curve 3D x = x (t), y = y(t), z = z (t) t∈ [0, 2π]*
ezplot3(x, y,z, domain)	*Parametric curve 3D x = x (t), y = y(t), z = z (t) t∈ domain*
ezplot3(..., 'animate')	*Parametric curve for 3D animation*
ezpolar(f)	*Graph the polar curve r = f(c) with c∈ [0, 2π]*
ezpolar(f, [a, b])	*Graph the polar curve r = f(c) with c∈ [a, b]*
pareto(Y)	*Makes the graphic relative to the Pareto values vector of frequencies and*
pareto(X,Y)	*Makes the graphic relative to the Pareto values vector whose elements are given by the vector X*
pie3(X)	*3-D pie frequenciesvalues chart for X*
pie3(X, explode)	*Detached three-dimensional pie chart*
plotmatrix(X, Y)	*Scatter graph of the columns of X against Y*

(continued)

quiver(U,V) **quiver(X, Y, U, V)** **quiver(..., scale)** **quiver(..., LineSpec)** **quiver(..., LineSpec, 'filled')**	*Graph of velocity of the vectors with components (u, v) in the points (x, y). You can define a scale, specifications, line and fill.*
ribbon(y) **ribbon(X, Y)** **ribbon(X, Y, width)**	*Graphic with three-dimensional tapes as columns.* *Graph X against the columns of Y.* *Specifies the width of the tape.*
stairs(Y) **stairs(X, Y)** **stairs(...,LineSpec)**	*Stairstep graphic with elements of Y.* *Stairstep graphic with elements of Y corresponding with X.* *When the LineSpec parameter is used, colors can be controlled using 'r'=red, and so on.*
scatter(X,Y,S,C) **scatter(X,Y)** **scatter(X,Y,S)** **scatter(..., marker)** **scatter(..., 'filled')**	*Dispersion for the vector graph (X, Y) according to color C and the area of each marker S. You can also get the graphic filled (fill option) and use different types of markers.*
scatter3(X,Y,Z,S,C) **scatter3(X,Y,Z)** **scatter3(X,Y,Z,S)** **scatter3(...,marker)** **scatter(...,'filled')**	*Graphic three-dimensional scatter (X, Y, Z) vectors according to the colors C and the area of each marker S. You can also get the graphic filled (fill option) and use different types of markers.*
TRI = delaunay(x,y)	*Delaunay Triangulation.*
K = dsearch(x,y,TRI,xi,yi)	*Delaunay Triangulation for the nearest point.*
IN = inpolygon(X,Y,xv,yv)	*Detects points inside a polygonal region.*
polyarea(X, Y)	*Area of the polygon specified by vectors X and Y.*
tsearch	*Delaunay Triangulation.*
voronoi(x,y) **voronoi(x, y, TRI)**	*Voronoi diagrams.*

As a first example, we carry out a stacked area chart (see Figure 4-17).

```
>> Y = [1, 5, 3;
3, 2, 7;
1, 5, 3;
2, 6, 1];
area(Y)
grid on
colormap summer
```

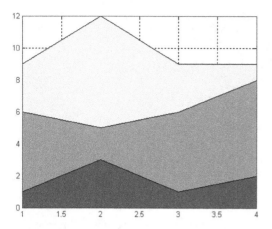

Figure 4-17.

We then create a two-dimensional Comet graph (Figure 4-18).

```
>> t = 0:.01:2 * pi;
x = cos(2*t) .* (cos (t) .^ 2);
y = sin(2*t) .* (sin (t) .^ 2);
comet(x,y);
```

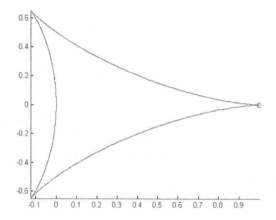

Figure 4-18.

Then is the contour graphic (Figure 4-19) for the function:

$$f(x,y)=3(1-x)^2 e^{-x^2}-(y+1)^2-10\left(\frac{x}{5}-x^3-y^5\right)e^{-x^2-y^2}-\frac{1}{3}e^{-(x+1)^2}-y^2$$

```
>> f = ['3 *(1-x)^2 * exp (-(x^2)-(y + 1)^2)','-10 *(x/5-x^3-y^5) * exp(-x^2-y^2)',
'-1/3 * exp (-(x + 1)^2 - y^2)'];

>> ezcontour(f,[-3,3],49)
```

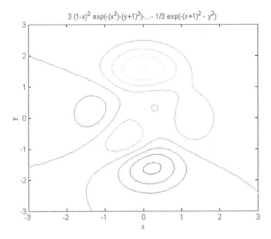

Figure 4-19.

Then we fill the color in the previous contour (Figure 4-20).

```
>> ezcontourf(f,[-3,3],49)
```

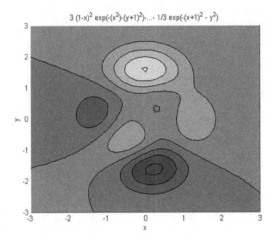

Figure 4-20.

In the following example we do a mixed mesh-contour (Figure 4-21) for the function chart:

$$f(x,y)=\frac{y}{1+x^2+y^2}$$

```
>> ezmeshc('y /(1 + x^2 + y^2)', [- 5, 5 - 2 * pi, 2 * pi])
colormap jet
```

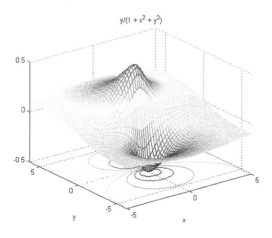

Figure 4-21.

Then the graphical surface and contour (Figure 4-22).

```
>> ezsurfc('y/(1 + x^2 + y^2)', [- 5, 5 - 2 * pi, 2 * pi], 35)
```

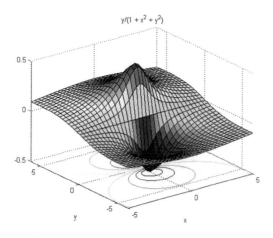

Figure 4-22.

Then graph a curve in parametric space (Figure 4-23).

```
>> ezplot3('sin(t)','cos(t)','t',[0,6*pi])
```

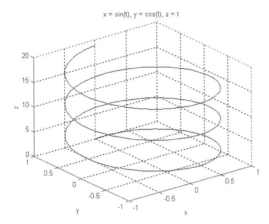

Figure 4-23.

The following example builds a graph in three-dimensional sectors (Figure 4-24).

```
>> x = [1 3 0.5 2.5 2];
explode = [0 1 0 0 0];
pie3(x, explode)
colormap hsv
```

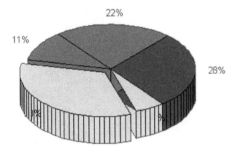

Figure 4-24.

Then create a tape chart for surface *peaks* (Figure 4-25).

```
>> [x, y] = meshgrid(-3:.5:3,-3:.1:3);
z = peaks(x,y);
ribbon(y, z)
colormap hsv
```

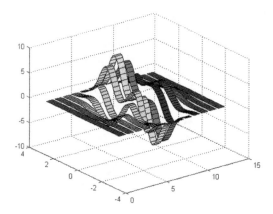

Figure 4-25.

The following example creates a stepped flat graph (Figure 4-26).

```
>> x = 0:.25:10;
stairs(x,sin(x))
```

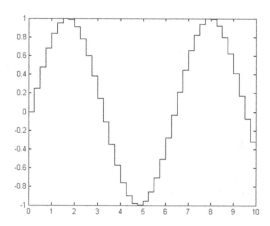

Figure 4-26.

The following code creates a graph of a three-dimensional scatter plot (Figure 4-27).

```
>> [x, y, z] = sphere(16);
X = [x(:) *.5 x(:) *.75 x(:)];
Y = [y(:) *.5 y(:) *.75 y(:)];
Z = [z(:) *.5 z(:) *.75 z(:)];
S = repmat([1 0.75 0.5] * 10, prod(size(x)),1);
C = repmat([1 2 3],prod(size(x)),1);
scatter3(X(:),Y(:),Z(:),S(:),C(:),'filled'), view(-60,60)
```

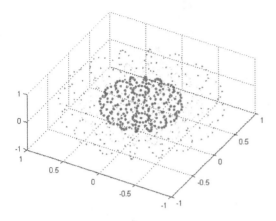

Figure 4-27.

Below is a polygonal area (Figure 4-28).

```
>> L = linspace(0,2.*pi,6); xv = cos(L)'; yv = sin(L)';
xv = [xv; xv(1)]; yv = [yv ; yv(1)];
A = polyarea(xv,yv);
plot(xv,yv); title(['Area = ' num2str(A)]); axis image
```

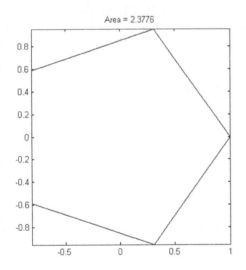

Figure 4-28.

4.3 Special 3D Geometric Shapes

MATLAB provides commands to represent geometric shapes in three dimensions, such as cylinders, spheres, rods, sections, stems, waterfall, etc. The syntax of these commands is presented in the following table:

bar3(Y)	*Bar graph relative to the frequencies values vector Y. If a matrix it gets multiple bar graphs for each row of Y.*
bar3(x,Y)	*Bar graph relative to the values vector Y where x is a vector that defines the spaces in the x axis to locate bars.*
bar3(...,width)	*Graph with given width of the bars. By default, the width is 0.8 and a width of 1 causes bars that touch.*
bar3(...,'style')	*Graph with the given style bars. The styles are 'detached' (default style) 'grouped' (style with grouped vertical bars) and 'stacked' (stacked bars).*
bar3(...,color)	*The bars are all of the specified color (r = red, g = green, b = blue, c = cyan, m = magenta y = yellow, k = black and w = white)*
comet3(z)	*Graph relative to the Comet vector z*
comet3(x, y, z)	*Comet graph with parameters (x (t), y (t), z (t))*
comet3(x, y, z, p)	*Comet graph of a kite with body of length p * length (y).*
[X, Y, Z] = cylinder	*It gives the coordinates of the unit cylinder.*
[X, Y, Z] = cylinder(r)	*It gives the coordinates of the cylinder generated by the curve r.*
[X,Y, Z] = cylinder(r, n)	*Gives the coordinates of the cylinder generated by the curve r with n points on the circumference that align the horizontal section with the Z axis (n = 20 by default).*
cylinder(...)	*Graph previous cylinders.*
sphere	*Graph the unit sphere using 20 x 20 faces.*
sphere(n)	*Generates a sphere using n x n.*
[X, Y, Z] = sphere(n)	*Gives the coordinates of the sphere in three arrays (n + 1) x (n + 1).*
slice(V,sx,sy,sz)	*Draws slices along directions x, y and z in the volume V (array m x n x p) defined by the vectors (sx, sy, sz).*
slice(X,Y,Z,V,sx,sy,sz)	*Draws cuts defined by the vectors (sx, sy, sz) in the volume V, defined by the three-dimensional arrays (X, Y, Z).*
slice(V,XI,YI,ZI)	*Draws cuts in volume V defined by (XI, YI, ZI) matrices that generate a surface.*
slice(X,Y,Z,V,XI,YI,ZI)	*Draws cuts defined by (XI, YI, ZI) matrices that generate a surface in the volume V, defined by the three-dimensional arrays (X, Y, Z).*
slice(...,'method')	*Draws cuts according to the specified method of interpolation (linear, cubic and nearest).*
stem3(Z)	*Draws the sequence Z as a graph of stems in the plane (x, y).*
stem3(X,Y,Z)	*Draws the sequence of values specified by X, Y and Z.*
stem3(...,'fill')	*Fill color in the circles at the tips of the stems.*
stem3(...,S)	*Makes stems utilize S specifications chart (color,...).*
waterfall(X,Y,Z)	*Draws a cascade graph according to the values of X, Y, Z.*
waterfall(Z)	*This means x = 1:size(Z,2) and y = 1:size(Z,1).*
waterfall(...,C)	*Draws the cascade graph with colormap C.*
quiver3(X,Y,Z,U,V,W)	*Draws the vectors of components (u, v, w) in the points (x, y, z).*

The first example presents a chart with various kinds of subgraphs (Figure 4-29) as three-dimensional bar charts.

```
>> Y = cool(7);
subplot(3,2,1)
bar3(Y,'detached')
title('Detached')

subplot(3,2,2)
bar3(Y,0.25,'detached')
title('Width = 0.25')

subplot(3,2,3)
bar3(Y,'grouped')
title('Grouped')

subplot(3,2,4)
bar3(Y,0.5,'grouped')
title('Width = 0.5')

subplot(3,2,5)
bar3(Y,'stacked')
title('Stacked')

subplot(3,2,6)
bar3(Y,0.3,'stacked')
title('Width = 0.3')
```

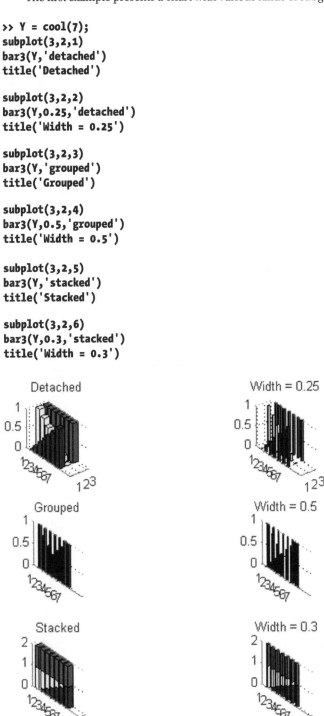

Figure 4-29.

The following example creates a three-dimensional kite graph (Figure 4-30).

```
>> t = - 10 * pi: pi / 250:10 * pi;
comet3((cos(2*t) .^ 2) .* sin(t),(sin(2*t) .^ 2) .* cos(t),t);
```

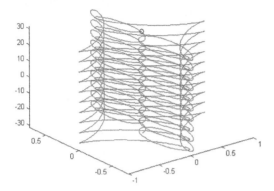

Figure 4-30.

The following is the syntax that creates a graph of stems to display a function of two variables (Figure 4-31).

```
>> X = linspace(0,1,10);
Y = X / 2;
Z = sin (X) + cos (Y);
stem3(X,Y,Z,'fill')
```

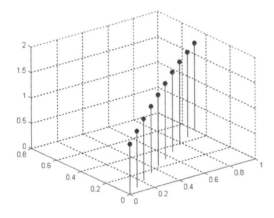

Figure 4-31.

Then draw the field unit with equal axes (Figure 4-32).

```
>> sphere
axis equal
```

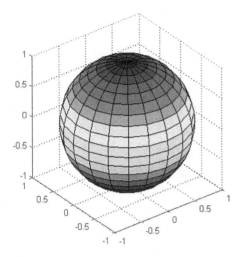

Figure 4-32.

Finally draw the cylinder unit within a square axis (Figure 4-33).

```
>> cylinder
axis square
```

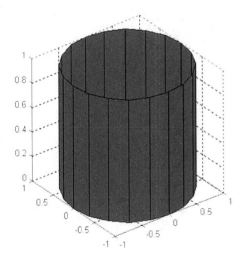

Figure 4-33.

4.4 Print, Export and Other Tasks with Graphics

The following table presents several commands of MATLAB which enable you to print graphics, select printer options and save graphics files.

orient	*Situates the paper orientation for printing on your value by default.*
orient landscape	*Situates the horizontal print orientation.*
orient portrait	*Situated the vertical print orientation.*
orient tall	*Prints the entire page with portrait orientation.*
pagesetupdlg	*Presents a dialog box to manage the position of the picture.*
print	*Prints the chart using hardcopy.*
print -*device options* file	*Print the graph to a file with given device options.*
printdlg	*Prints the current figure.*
printdlg(fig)	*Creates a dialog for printing identified by fig.*
saveas(h,'file.ext')	*Save figure h in the graphic file file.ext.*
saveas(h,'file','format')	*File guardian figure h in the file with the specified graphic format.*

According to extension, the graphic file formats are as follows:

Extension	Format
AI	*Adobe Illustrator' 88*
BMP	*Windows bitmap*
EMF	*Enhanced metafile*
EPS	*EPS Level 1*
Fig	*MATLAB figure*
jpg	*JPEG image*
m	*MATLAB M-file*
PBM	*Portable bitmap*
PCX	*Paintbrush 24-bit*
PGM	*Portable Graymap*
PNG	*Portable Network Graphics*
ppm	*Portable Pixmap*
TIF	*Image TIFF compressed image*

CHAPTER 5

■ ■ ■

Graphics Special Commands

5.1 Two Dimensional Graphics: FPLOT and EZPLOT

Commands *fplot* and *ezplot* graph curves using commands developed for a wide array of cases without having to specify all the details built in every time. Their syntax is as follows:

fplot('f', [xmin, xmax])	*Graphs the function between the limits in each case given in this table.*
fplot('f',[xmin, xmax, ymin, ymax], S)	*Graphs the function at intervals of variation of x and y, with options for color and characters given by S. ymin and ymax control the values of the vertical axis.*
fplot('[f1,f2,...,fn]',[xmin, xmax, ymin, ymax], S,t,n)	*Graphs functions f1, f2,..., fn on the same axes in the ranges of variation of x and specified with the options for color and characters defined in S*
fplot('f',[xmin, xmax],...,t)	*Graphs of f using the tolerance t*
fplot('f',[xmin, xmax],...,n)	*Graphs of f where n> = 1*
ezplot('f', [xmin, xmax])	*Similar to fplot*
ezplot('f', [xmin, xmax, ymin, ymax])	*Graphs the function f(x,y) at given intervals of variation of x and y . Unlike fplot, ezplot can be f(x,y)*
ezplot(x, y)	*Graphs the planar parametric curve x = x(t) and y = y(t) on the domain 0 < t < 2π*
ezplot('f', [xmin, xmax])	*Graphs the planar parametric curve x = x(t) and y = y(t).* This is a variation on ezplot(x,y) which expects two function parameters; the only difference here is that tmin and tmax are used instead of the implied 0 to 2pi. So, the syntax is ezplot(fx,fy,[tmin tmax])
ezplot('f')	*Graphs curve f in implicit in [-2π, 2π]*

As a first example, perform the graph of the function $f(x) = Sin(x)e^{-0.4x}$ over the range [0,10]. Figure 5-1 presents the results of the following syntax:

```
>> x = 0:0.05:10;
>> y = sin(x) .* exp(-0.4*x);
>> plot(x,y)
```

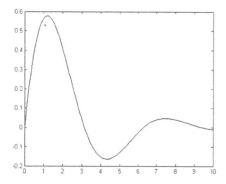

Figure 5-1.

The representation of the previous curve (Figure 5-2) can also be done using the following syntax:

```
>> ezplot('sin(x) * exp(-0.4*x)', [0,10])
```

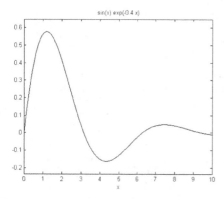

Figure 5-2.

Note that ezplot automatically sets the title. You could also obtain the same graphical representation using the following command:

```
>> fplot('sin(x) * exp(-0.4*x)', [0,10])
```

Figure 5-3 shows the curve for $x^2 - y^4 = 0$ in the range $[-2\pi, 2\pi]$ using the following syntax:

```
>> ezplot('x^2-y^4')
```

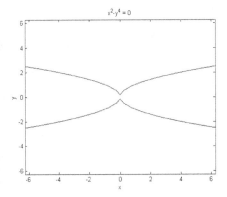

Figure 5-3.

Then we graph the parametric curve- $x(t) = 4cos(t) - cos(4t)$, $y(t) = 4sin(t) - sin(4t)$ varying t between 0 and 2π (Figure 5-4). The syntax is as follows:

```
>> t = 0:0.1:2*pi;
>> x = 4 * cos(t) - cos(4*t);
>> y = 4 * sin(t) - sin(4*t);
>> plot(x,y)
```

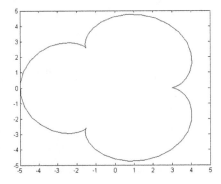

Figure 5-4.

The same graph (Figure 5-5) could have been obtained by using the following syntax:

```
>> ezplot('4*cos(t) - cos(4*t)', '4*sin(t) - sin(4*t)', [0, 2*pi])
```

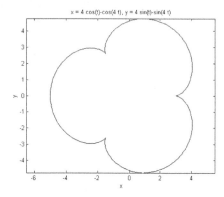

Figure 5-5.

Next, were present the curves *Sine* (*x*), *Sine* (2*x*) and *Sine* (3*x*) about the same axes as shown in Figure 5-6. The syntax is as follows:

```
>> fplot('[sin(x), sin(2*x), sin(3*x)]', [0, 2*pi])
```

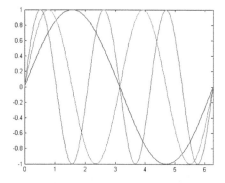

Figure 5-6.

We can try to represent every previous curve using different strokes (Figure 5-7) by using the following syntax:

```
>> fplot('[sin(x), sin(2*x), sin(3*x)]', [0, 2*pi],'*')
```

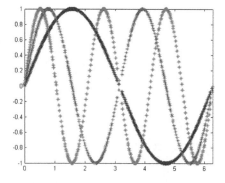

Figure 5-7.

Below you will find the syntax used to represent the polar curve $r = Sin\,(2a)\,Cos\,(2a)$ for t between 0 and 2π (Figure 5-8).

```
>> t = 0:0.1:2*pi;
>> r = sin(2*t).* cos(2*t);
>> polar(t,r)
```

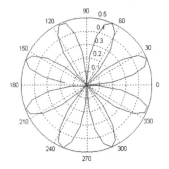

Figure 5-8.

This example could also represent this polar curve with a dashed line of red color (Figure 5-9) using the following syntax:

```
>> t = 0:0.1:2*pi;
>> r = sin(2*t).*cos(2*t);
>> polar(t,r,'--r')
```

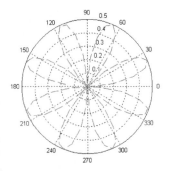

Figure 5-9.

5.2 Three-Dimensional Graphics with EZ Command

In the same way that ez functions are used to represent two-dimensional graphics without specifying the field of existence of an array form, three-dimensional graphics of warped curves, surfaces, contour lines, contour and other types of graphics can also be used, the commands to use are as follows:

ezcontour(f)	*Contour graph of f(x,y) in [-2π, 2π] x [-2π, 2π]*
ezcontour(f, domain)	*Contour graph of f(x,y) in the given domain*
ezcontour(...,n)	*Contour graph of f(x,y) in mesh of size n x n*
ezcontourf(f)	*Filling contour graph of f(x,y) in [-2π, 2π] x [-2π, 2π]*
ezcontourf(f, domain)	*Filling contour graph of f(x, y) in the given domain*
ezcontourf(...,n)	*Contour graph of f(x, y) filling in a n x n mesh*
ezmesh(f)	*Filling mesh graph of f(x,y) at [-2π, 2π] x [-2π, 2π]*
ezmesh(f,domain)	*Filling mesh raph of f(x,y) in the given domain*
ezmesh(...,n)	*Filling Mesh graph of f(x,y) in the nxn mesh*
ezmesh(x, y, z)	*Mesh graph for x = x(t,u), y = y(t,u), z = z(t,u) where t,u∈ [-2π, 2π]*
ezmesh(x, y, z, domain)	*Mesh graph for x = x(t,u), y = y(t,u), z = z(t,u) where t,u∈ domain*
ezmesh(..., 'circ')	*Mesh graph of a circle, not the default square, centered in the domain*
ezmeshc(f)	*Performs a combination of mesh and contour graph elements*
ezmeshc(f, domain)	
ezmeshc(...,n)	
ezmeshc(x, y, z)	
ezmeshc(x, and z, domain)	
ezmeshc(..., 'circ')	
ezsurf(f)	*These make a colored surface chart*
ezsurf(f, domain)	
ezsurf(...,n)	
ezsurf(x, y, z)	
ezsurf (x, y, z, domain)	
ezsurf(..., 'circ')	
ezsurfc(f)	*This creates diagrams that are a combination of surface and contour graphs*
ezsurfc(f, domain)	
ezsurfc(...,n)	
ezsurfc(x, y, z)	
ezsurfc(x, y, z, domain)	
ezsurfc(..., 'circ')	
ezplot3(x, y, z)	*Parametric curve in 3D for x = x(t), y = y(t), z = z(t) t∈ [-2π, 2π]*
ezplot3(x, y, z, domain)	*Parametric curve in 3D for x = x(t), y = y(t), z = z(t) t∈domain*
ezplot3(..., 'animate')	*Parametric curve using 3D animation*
ezpolar(f)	*Graph the polar curve r = f(c) with c∈ [0, 2π]*
ezpolar(f, [a, b])	*Graph the polar curve r = f(c) with c∈ [a, b]*

Below is the contour graph (Figure 5-10) for the function:

$$f(x,y) = 3(1-x)^2 e^{-x^2-(y+1)^2} - 10\left(\frac{x}{5} - x^3 - y^5\right)e^{-x^2-y^2} - \frac{1}{3}e^{-(x+1)^2-y^2}$$

```
>> f = ['3 *(1-x)^2*exp(-(x^2)-(y + 1)^2)',...
'-10*(x/5-x^3-y^5)*exp(-x^2-y^2)','-1/3*exp(-(x + 1)^2 - y^2)'];

>> ezcontour(f,[-3,3],49)
   colormap summer
```

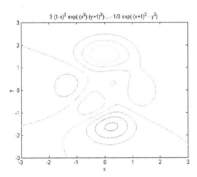

Figure 5-10.

Then fill in color in the previous contour (Figure 5-11).

```
>> ezcontourf(f,[-3,3],49)
```

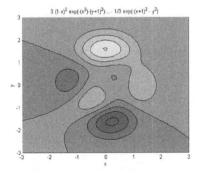

Figure 5-11.

In the following example we do a mixed mesh-contour (Figure 5-12) for the chart function:

$$f(x,y) = \frac{y}{1+x^2+y^2}$$

```
>> ezmeshc('y /(1 + x^2 + y^2)', [- 5, 5, - 2*pi, 2*pi])
```

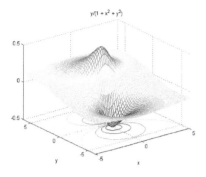

Figure 5-12.

Later is a graphical surface and contour (Figure 5-13).

```
>> ezsurfc('y/(1 + x^2 + y^2)', [- 5, 5, - 2*pi, 2*pi], 35)
```

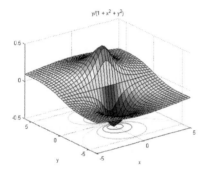

Figure 5-13.

Then we graph a curve in parametric space.

```
>> ezplot3('sin(t)', 'cos(t)',', [0, 6 * pi])
```

EXERCISE 5-1

Represent the following function in the interval [−8.8]

$$f(x) = \frac{x^3}{x^2 - 4}$$

Figure 5-14 represents the function by using the following syntax:

```
>> ezplot('x^3 / (x^2-4)', [-8, 8])
```

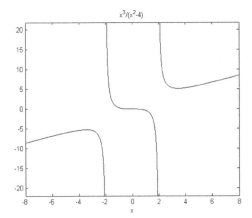

Figure 5-14.

EXERCISE 5-2

Graph, on the same axes, the functions bessel(1,x), bessel(2,x) and bessel(3,x) for values of x between 0 and 12, evenly spaced using two-tenths. Place three legends and add three different types of strokes (normal, asterisks and circles, respectively) to the three functions.

Figure 5-15 represents the capabilities requested by using the following syntax:

```
>> x = 0:.2:12;
plot(x, besselj(1,x), x, besselj(2,x),'*', x, besselj(3,x), 'o');
legend('Bessel(1,x)', 'Bessel(2,x)', 'Bessel(3,x)');
```

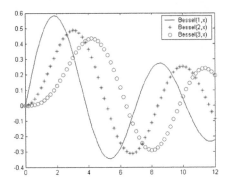

Figure 5-15.

EXERCISE 5-3

Represent the polar curve $r = 4 (1 + Cos (a))$ between 0 and 2π (cardioid). Also represent the curve in polar, $r = 3a$ for a between $- 4\pi$ and 4π (spiral).

The first curve (Figure 5-16) is represented using the following syntax:

```
>> a = 0:0.01:2*pi;
r = 4 * (1 + cos(a));
polar(a, r)
title('CARDIOID')
```

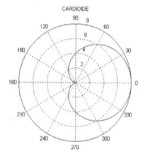

Figure 5-16.

The second curve (Figure 5-17) can be represented using the syntax:

```
>> ezpolar('3*a',[-4*pi,4*pi])
```

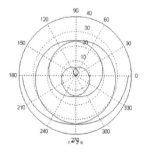

Figure 5-17.

EXERCISE 5-4

Represent the warped curve of parametric coordinates, $x = \text{Cos}^2(t)$, $y = \text{Sine }(t) \cos(t)$, $z = \text{Sine }(t)$ for t ranging from -4π to 4π.

Figure 5-18 represents the capabilities requested by using the following syntax:

```
>> t = -4 * pi: 0.01:4 * pi;
x = cos(t) .^ 2;
y = sin(t) .* cos(t);
z = sin(t);
plot3(x, y, z)
```

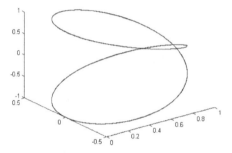

Figure 5-18.

EXERCISE 5-5

Represent the surface, your mesh graph and the contour graph whose equation is as follows:

$$z = xe^{-x^2-y^2} \quad -2 < x, y < 2$$

The graph of the surface (Figure 5-19) can be represented as follows:

```
>> ezsurf('x * exp(-x^2-y^2)', [- 2, 2], [- 2, 2])
```

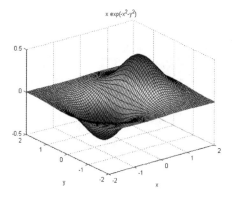

Figure 5-19.

The mesh (Figure 5-20) graph can be represented as follows:

```
>> ezmesh('x * exp(-x^2-y^2)', [- 2, 2], [- 2, 2])
```

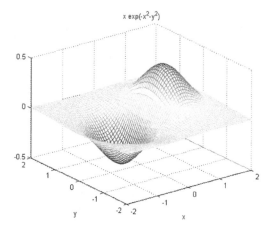

Figure 5-20.

The contour graph (Figure 5-21) can be represented as follows:

```
>> ezcontour('x * exp(-x^2-y^2)', [-2, 2], [-2, 2])
```

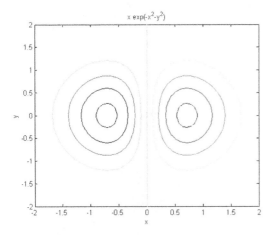

Figure 5-21.

We can make the graph of the surface and contour simultaneously (Figure 5-22) as follows:

```
>> ezsurfc('x * exp(-x^2-y^2)', [- 2, 2], [- 2, 2])
```

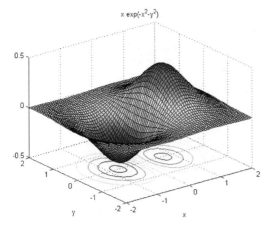

Figure 5-22.

We can make the mesh-contour chart simultaneously (Figure 5-23) as follows:

```
>> ezmeshc('x * exp(-x^2-y^2)', [- 2, 2], [- 2, 2])
```

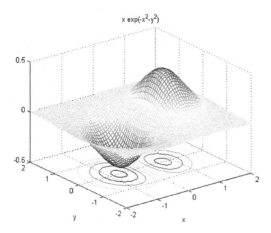

Figure 5-23.

We can also represent the mesh graph with the option of curtain or curtain bottom (Figure 5-24) as follows:

```
>> [X, Y] = meshgrid(-2:.1:2,-2:.1:2);
Z = X .* exp(-X.^2-Y.^2);
meshz(X, Y, Z)
```

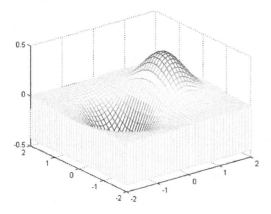

Figure 5-24.

5.3 Steps to Graphing Data

As we have seen, the Basic module of MATLAB offers a wide range of options when it comes to graphic representations. It allows graphs of planar curves and surfaces, enabling grouping and overlapping. It is also possible to work colors, grids, frames, etc., into the graphics. Representations of functions can be in implicit, explicit and parametric coordinates. MATLAB is therefore mathematical software with high graphics performance, distinguishing it from many other symbolic calculation packages. MATLAB also allows graphics of bars, lines, stars, histograms, polyhedra, geographical maps and animations. The creation of a graph is usually attached to the following steps:

Step	Example
Prepare the data	`x = 0:0.2:12; Y1 = besselj(1,x);` `Y2 = besselj(2,x); Y3 = besselj(3,x);`
Choose the window and locate the position	`figure(1); subplot(2,2,1)`
Use a graphic function	`h = plot(x,Y1,x,Y2,x,Y3);`
Choose lines and markercharacteristics (width, colors,...)	`set(h,'LineWidth',2,{'LineStyle'});` `set(h,{'Color'},{'r';'g';'b'})`
Position limits of axes, marks and mesh	`axis([0,12,-0.5,1]) grid on`

Place annotations, labels, and legends	`xlabel('Time'); ylabel('Amplitude')`
	`legend(h,'First','Second','Third')`
	`title('Bessel Functions')`
	`[y,ix] = min(Y1);`

Export the graph	`print -depsc -tiff -r200 graphname`

5.4 Steps to Perform 3 –D Graphics

The Basic module of MATLAB allows graphics in three dimensions, both lines and nets and surfaces. You can also use explicit and parametric coordinates. The steps followed in general to carry out a three-dimensional graph are presented in the following table:

Step	Example
1. Prepare the data	`Z = peaks(20);`
2. Select the window and position	`figure(1)` `subplot(2,1,2)`
3. Use a 3-D graphic function	`h = surf(Z);`

4. Place color and shadow	`colormap hot`
	`shading interp`
	`set(h,'EdgeColor','k')`

5. Add lighting	`light('Position',[-2,2,20])`
	`lighting phong`
	`material([0.4,0.6,0.5,30])`
	`set(h,'FaceColor',[0.7 0.7 0],...`
	`        'BackFaceLighting','lit')`

(*continued*)

Step	Example
6. Place the point of view	`view([30,25])` `set(gca,'CameraViewAngleMode','Manual')`
7. Position limits and markings on shafts	`axis([5 15 5 15 -8 8])` `set(gca,'ZTickLabel','Negative||Positive')`
8. Set the aspect ratio	`set(gca, 'PlotBoxAspectRatio', [2.5 2.5 1])`

9. Place annotationslegends, chart and axes	`xlabel('X Axis')`
	`ylabel('Y Axis')`
	`zlabel('Function Value')`
	`title('Peaks')`

10. Print the chart	`set(gcf,'PaperPositionMode','auto')` `print -dps2`

You can use some or all of these steps to create your graphic. So let's go through a few examples. As a first example we consider the surface $z = x^2 - y^2$ in $[-2,2]$ x $[-2,2]$ and represent it with strong lighting, shading dense grayish colors (Figure 5-25).

```
>> [X, and] = meshgrid(-2:0.05:2);
Z = X .^ 2 - Y .^ 2;
surf(X,Y,Z),shading interp,brighten(0.75),colormap(gray(5))
```

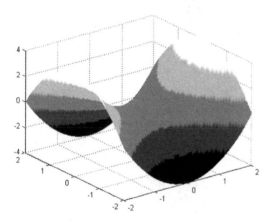

Figure 5-25.

Then we represent, on the same axes, the curve focused from four different points of view and with shading by default (Figure 5-26).

```
>> [X, Y] = meshgrid(-2:0.05:2);
Z = X .^ 2 - Y .^ 2;
subplot(2,2,1)
surf(X,Y,Z)
subplot(2,2,2)
```

```
surf(X,Y,Z),view(-90,0)
subplot(2,2,3)
surf(X,Y,Z),view(60,30)
subplot(2,2,4)
surf(X,Y,Z),view(-10,30)
```

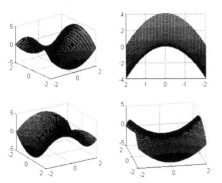

Figure 5-26.

Then MATLAB reads a file and appropriate properties are used to generate the colorful graph in Figure 5-27.

```
>> load clown
surface(peaks,flipud(X),...
'FaceColor','texturemap',...
'EdgeColor','none',...
'CDataMapping','direct')
colormap(map)
view(-35, 45)
```

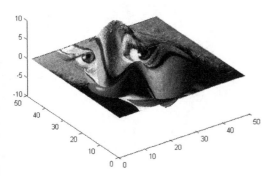

Figure 5-27.

Our clown could use a ball, so let's create one for him. Different shaders are used for the sphere (Figure 5-28).

```
>> subplot(3,1,1)
sphere(16)
axis square
shading flat
title('Soft shading')

subplot(3,1,2)
sphere(16)
axis square
shading faceted
title(' Normal shading')

subplot(3,1,3)
sphere(16)
axis square
shading interp
title('Dense shading')
```

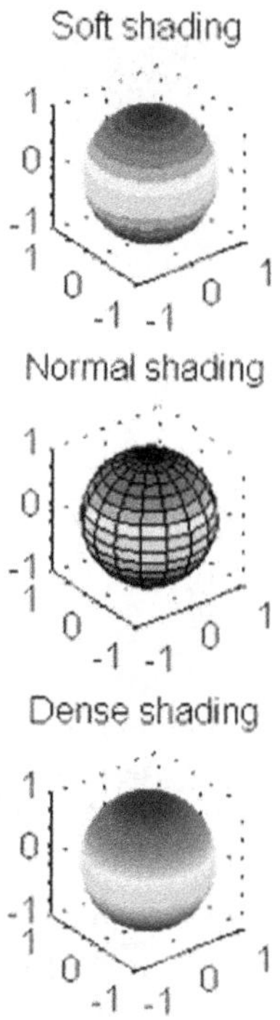

Figure 5-28.

The following example changes the ratio of appearance for the sphere (Figure 5-29).

```
>> sphere
set(gca,'DataAspectRatio',[1 1 1],...
'PlotBoxAspectRatio',[1 1 1],'ZLim',[-0.6 0.6])
```

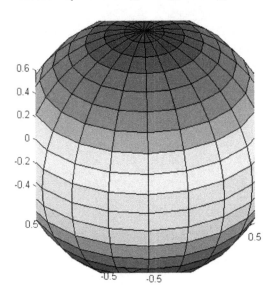

Figure 5-29.

Now place the background color of the current figure in white (Figure 5-30).

```
>> set(gcf, 'Color', 'w')
```

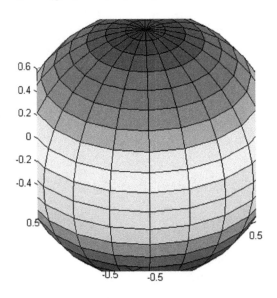

Figure 5-30.

In the following example (Figure 5-31), we represent a surface utilizing the function *peaks* predefined in MATLAB (similar to a two-dimensional Gaussian distribution) with change of origin and scale.

```
>> surf(peaks(20))
```

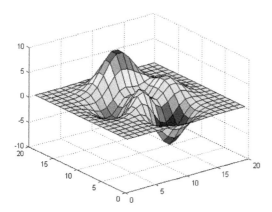

Figure 5-31.

Then we rotate the figure above 180 degrees around the axis X (Figure 5-32).

```
>> h = surf(peaks(20));
rotate(h,[1 0 0],15)
```

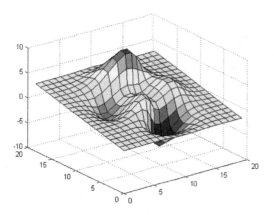

Figure 5-32.

Then we change the center and rotate the start surface 45° in the direction of the axis *z* (Figure 5-33).

```
>> h = surf(peaks(20));
zdir = [0 0 1];
center = [10 10 0];
rotate(h,zdir,45,center)
```

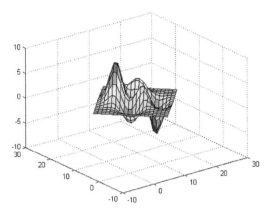

Figure 5-33.

In the following example we define several axes in a simple window (Figure 5-34).

```
>> axes('position',[.1  .1  .8  .6])
mesh(peaks(20));
axes('position',[.1  .7  .8  .2])
pcolor([1:10;1:10]);
```

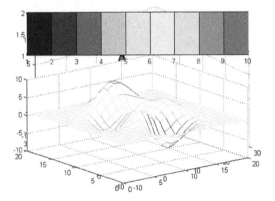

Figure 5-34.

Then we equip special lighting, grey dense shading and variation of axes in [- 3, 3] x [- 3, 3] x [- 8, 8] to the *peaks* surface (Figure 5-35).

```
>> [x, y] = meshgrid(-3:1/8:3);
z = peaks(x,y);
surfl(x,y,z);
shading interp
colormap (gray);
axis([-3 3,-3 3,-8 8])
```

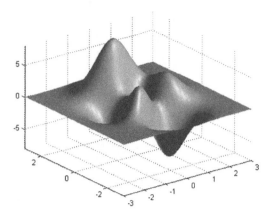

Figure 5-35.

Then we change perspective, mesh and color to the previous illuminated surface (Figure 5-36).

```
>> view([10 10])
grid on
hold on
surfl(peaks)
shading interp
colormap copper
hold off
```

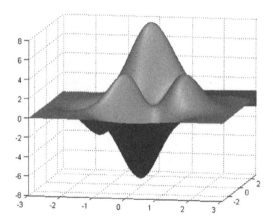

Figure 5-36.

Below are two examples of triangle graphics (Figures 5-37 and 5-38). Note that because the rand function is used, your results will not be the same as these.

```
>> x = rand(1,50);
y = rand(1,50);
z = peaks(6*x-3,6*x-3);
tri = delaunay(x,y);
trimesh(tri,x,y,z)
```

```
>> x = rand(1,50);
y = rand(1,50);
z = peaks(6*x-3,6*x-3);
tri = delaunay(x,y);
trisurf(tri,x,y,z);
colormap copper
```

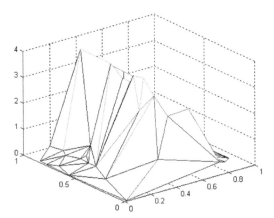

Figure 5-37.

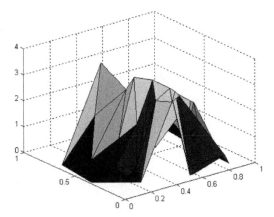

Figure 5-38.

As you can see from the examples in this chapter, you have many options at your disposal to enhance or modify your graphics to suit your needs.

CHAPTER 6

Polynomials and Graphics Interpolation

6.1 Polynomial Expressions

The content of this chapter refers to work with polynomials and polynomial interpolation. We will study the commands that enable MATLAB to perform all operations with polynomials, working with their roots and polynomial interpolation.

MATLAB enables several commands for handling algebraic polynomial expressions. Let's take a look at some of these commands:

conv(a, b) gives the vector with the coefficients of the product of polynomials whose coefficients are elements of the vectors *a* and *b*.

[q, r] = deconv(a, b) gives the vector *q* with the coefficients of the quotient of polynomials whose coefficients are elements of the vectors *a* and *b*, and the vector *r*, which is the polynomial remainder from division.

poly2sym(a) is a Symbolic toolbox function that generates an object of the sym class creating the polynomial whose coefficients are those specified in the vector *a*.

sym2poly(a) writes the vector of the specified polynomial coefficients (reverse operation to the previous one).

roots(a) gives the roots of the polynomial whose coefficients are the vector *a*.

poly(v) gives the polynomial whose roots are the components of the vector *v*.

poly(A) gives the characteristic polynomial matrix *A*.

polyder(a) gives the vector *a* whose coefficients are the first derivative of the polynomial.

polyder(a, b) gives the vector whose coefficients are the derivative of the polynomial product of *a* and *b*.

[q, d] = polyder(a, b) gives the coefficients of the numerator and denominator of the derivative of the polynomial quotient *a/b*.

polyval(p, x, S) evaluates the polynomial *p* in x with standard deviation of the error equal to *S*.

polyvalm(p, X) evaluates the polynomial p in matrix X.

[r, p, k] = residue(a, b) gives the column vectors r, p and k such that:

$b(s)/a(s)=r1/(s-p1)+r2/(s-p2)+...+rn/(s-pn)+k(s)$

[b, a] = residue(r, p, k) performs the reverse of the previous operation.

Then let's look at some examples of these newly defined commands:
Let's decompose the fraction $(-x \wedge 2 + 2x + 1)/(x\wedge2-1)$

```
>> [r,p,k]=residue([-1,2,1],[1,0,-1])

r =

1.0000
1.0000

p =

-1.0000
1.0000

k =

-1
```

So the decomposition will be:

$(-x \wedge 2 + 2x + 1)/(x\wedge2-1) = 1/(-1+x) + 1/(x+1) - 1$

The same result can be obtained in the following way:

```
>> pretty(sym(maple('convert((-x^2+2*x+1)/(x^2-1),parfrac,x)')))

          1        1
-1 + ---- + -----
          x      x + 1
```

Then we will evaluate the polynomial $x \wedge 4-6 * x \wedge 3-x \wedge 2 + 10 * x-11$ about the point $x = 5$ and on the matrix of order 4.

```
>> polyval([1,-6,-1,10,-11],5)

ans =

-111
```

```
>> polyvalm([1,-6,-1,10,-11],ones(4))
```

ans =

```
-37 -26 -26 -26
-26 -37 -26 -26
-26 -26 -37 -26
-26 -26 -26 -37
```

Now let's find the roots of the polynomial $x \wedge 3$-x:

```
>> roots([1,0,-1,0])
```

Ans =

```
0
-1.0000
1.0000
```

Now solve the equation $-x \wedge 5 + 2 * x \wedge 4 + x \wedge 3 + x \wedge 2 = 0$:

```
>> roots([-1,2,1,1,0,0])
```

ans =

```
0
0
2.5468
-0.2734 + 0.5638i
-0.2734 - 0.5638i
```

EXERCISE 6-1

We consider the polynomial's coefficients a = [2, -4, 5, 8, 0, 0, 1] and b = [-7, 15, 0, 12, 0]. Calculate the coefficients of the polynomials that are the product and quotient of a and b, also calculating the coefficients of the polynomials that are the derivatives of the products and the quotients of *a* and *b*.

```
>> a=[2,-4,5,8,0,0,1]; b=[-7,15,0,12,0];
```

```
>> conv(a,b)
```

ans =

```
-14    58    -95    43    72    60    89    15    0    12    0
```

```
>> [q,r]=deconv(a,b)
```

q =

```
-0.2857    -0.0408    -0.8017
```

r =

```
0        0        0    23.4548    0.4898    9.6210    1.0000
```

```
>> polyder(a)
```

ans =

```
12    -20    20    24    0    0
```

```
>> polyder(a,b)
```

ans =

```
-140 522 -760 301 432 300 356 45 0 12
```

```
>> [q, d] = polyder(a, b)
```

q =

```
-28 118 -120 251 -192 180 220 -45 0 -12
```

d =

```
49 -210 225 -168 360 0 144 0 0
```

The coefficient vectors can be transformed into the equivalent polynomials with the command *poly2sym*, resulting in polynomial form. Let's see:

The product polynomial will be:

```
>> pretty(poly2sym(conv(a, b)))
```

```
      10    9      8       7       6       5       4       3
-14 x + 58x - 95 x + 43 x + 72 x + 60 x + 89 x + 15 x + 12 x
```

The quotient polynomial is:

```
>> pretty(poly2sym(q))
```

```
        9         8        7         6        5         4         3        2
  - 28 x  + 118 x  - 120 x  + 251 x  - 192 x  + 180 x  + 220 x  - 45 x  - 12
```

The polynomial first derivative of a is:

```
>> pretty(poly2sym(polyder(a)))
```

$$12 \text{ x}^5 - 20 \text{ x}^4 + 20 \text{ x}^3 + 24 \text{ x}^2$$

The polynomial first derivative of the product of *a* and *b* is:

```
>> pretty(poly2sym(polyder(a,b)))
```

$$-140 \text{ x}^9 + 522 \text{ x}^8 - 760 \text{ x}^7 + 301 \text{ x}^6 + 432 \text{ x}^5 + 300 \text{ x}^4 + 356 \text{ x}^3 + 45 \text{ x}^2 + 12$$

The polynomial quotient *a/b* will be *q/d* where *q* and *d* are:

```
>> [q,d]=polyder(a,b);
>> pretty(poly2sym(q))
```

$$-28 \text{ x}^9 + 118 \text{ x}^8 - 120 \text{ x}^7 + 251 \text{ x}^6 - 192 \text{ x}^5 + 180 \text{ x}^4 + 220 \text{ x}^3 - 45 \text{ x}^2 - 12$$

```
>> pretty(poly2sym(d))
```

$$49 \text{ x}^8 - 210 \text{ x}^7 + 225 \text{ x}^6 - 168 \text{ x}^5 + 360 \text{ x}^4 + 144 \text{ x}^2$$

EXERCISE 6-2

Find the characteristic polynomial of the matrix whose rows are vectors [2, -4, 5, 8], [0, 0, 0, 1], [-7, 15, 0.12] and [0, -1, -1, 0]. Also find the roots of this polynomial and check that the matrix satisfies the equation of your characteristic polynomial.

```
>> A=[2,-4,5,8;0,0,0,1;-7,15,0,12;0,-1,-1,0]
```

A =

```
2    -4    5    8
0     0    0    1
-7    15   0   12
0    -1   -1    0
```

```
>> p=poly(A)
```

p =

```
1.0000   -2.0000   48.0000   -67.0000   33.0000
```

```
>> pretty(poly2sym(p))
```

```
   4     3       2
  x - 2x + 48 x - 67 x + 33
```

To find the roots of the characteristic polynomial we use:

```
>> roots(p)
```

ans =

```
0.2836 + 6.8115i
0.2836 - 6.8115i
0.7164 + 0.4435i
0.7164 - 0.4435i
```

To verify that the matrix A satisfies the characteristic polynomial, we find the values in the polynomial Matrix A and observe that the result almost generates the null matrix.

```
>> polyvalm(p,A)
```

ans =

```
  1.0e-012 *
```

```
 -0.1990    0.1137    0.0266    0.5969
  0.0093   -0.0711   -0.0071    0.0426
 -0.0870    0.1137   -0.4192   -0.3979
  0.0568   -0.1421    0.0013   -0.0497
```

EXERCISE 6-3

Expand the following operations in polynomial expressions.

```
        3 2           2 3 3
a) (5 x y z - 4 x y z)
```

```
        4     2 2     4
b) (x + y) (x + x y + y) (x - y)]
```

```
>> syms x y z
>> pretty(expand(simple(5*x^3*y^2*z-4*x*y^2*z^3)^3))
```

```
           9 6 3        7 6 5         5 6 7       3 6 9
      125 x y z - 300 x y z + 240 x y z - 64 x y z
```

```
>> pretty(expand((x+y) *(x^4+x^2*y^2+y^4) * (x-y)))
```

$$x^6 - y^6$$

This shows that the polynomial presents difficulties of expansion when you use only the command *expand*.

EXERCISE 6-4

Factorize as much as possible the following polynomial expressions.

a. $4x^2 + y^2 t^2 + z^4 - 4xyt + 4xz^2 - 2ytz$

b. $x^4 - x^2y^2 + 2xy^2 + x^2 - 2x^3 - y^2$

c. $amx + amy - bmx - bmy + bnx - anx - any + bny$

```
>> syms x y z b m n t
>> pretty(factor(4*x^2+y^2*t^2+z^4-4*x*y*t+4*x*z^2-2*y*t*z^2))
```

$$(2x - yt + z^2)^2$$

```
>> pretty(factor(x^4-x^2*y^2+2*x*y^2+x^2-2*x^3-y^2))
```

$$(x - 1)^2 (x - y) (x + y)$$

```
>> pretty(factor(a*m*x+a*m*y-b*m*x-b*m*y+b*n*x-a*n*x-a*n*y+b*n*y))
```

$$(x + y) (m - n) (a - b)$$

In general, in polynomial expressions, the command *expand* performs operations and simplifies the result, and the command *factor* factors the most.

```
>> pretty(expand((x-1)^2*(x-y)*(x+y)))
```

$$x^4 - 2x^3 - x^2y^2 + x^2 + 2xy^2 - y^2$$

6.2 Interpolation and Polynomial Fit

MATLAB provides several commands for polynomial interpolation and adjustment curves that we will study below:

polyfit(x, y, n) gives the vector of coefficients of the polynomial in x, $p(x)$ of degree n that best fits the data *(xi, yi)* in the least squares sense *(p(xi) = yi)*.

Yí = interp1(X,Y,Xi, 'method') gives the vector *Yi* such that *(Xi, Yi)* is the total set of points found by interpolation between the given points *(X, Y)*. The option *method* can take the value *linear, spline*, or *cubic*, depending on whether the interpolation is linear (default option), staggered or cubic (*Xi* points uniformly separated). This is for interpolation in one dimension.

Zi = interp2(X,Y,Z,Xi,Yi, 'method') gives *Zi* where *(Xi, Yi, Zi)* is the total set of points found by interpolation between the given points *(X, Y, Z)*. The option *method* can take the value *linear* or *cubic*, depending on whether the interpolation is linear (option by default) or cubic (*Xi* points uniformly separated). This is for two-dimensional interpolation.

Zi = griddata(X,Y,Z,Xi,Yi) gives the vector *Zi* that determines the interpolation points *(Xi, Yi, Zi)* between the given points *(X, Y, Z)*. A method of inverse distance is used to interpolate.

Y = interpft(X,n) gives the vector Y uses the values of the periodic function X sampled at n equally spaced points. The original vector x is transformed to the domain of frequencies of a Fourier transform using the Fast Fourier transform (FFT algorithm). Valid for $n \geq length\ (X)$.

maple('interp([exprx$_1$,...,exprx$_{n+1}$], [expry$_1$,...,expry$_{n+1}$],variable)') gives a polynomial in the specified variable of degree at least n that represents the interpoltion polynomial for points from *[exprx$_1$, expry$_1$]* to *[exprxexpry$_{n+1n+1}$]*. The coordinates of the points all have to be different.

maple('Interp([exprx$_1$,...,exprx$_{n+1}$], [expry$_1$,...,expry$_{n+1}$], variable)') in inert mode, is a polynomial in the specified variable of degree at least n that represents the interpolation polynomial for points from *[exprx$_1$, expry$_1$]* to *[exprx$_{n+1}$ expry$_{n+1}$]*. The coordinates of the points all have to be different.

maple('Interp([exprx$_1$,...,exprx$_{n+1}$], [expry$_1$,...,expry$_{n+1}$], variable) mod n') in inert mode Module-n, is a polynomial in the specified variable of degree at least n that represents the interpolation polynomial for points from *[exprx$_1$, expry$_1$]* to *[exprx$_{n+1}$ expry$_{n+1}$]*. The coordinates of the points all have to be different.

maple('readlib (thiele): thiele([exprx1,...,exprxn],[expry1,...,expryn],variable)') finds an expression in the given variable that represents the entire function resulting in the Thiele interpolation points *(exprxi, expryi) for i = 1... n*.

EXERCISE 6-5

Calculate the second degree interpolation polynomial passing through the points (-1,4), (0,2), and (1,6) in the least squares sense.

```
>> x=[-1,0,1];y=[4,2,6];p=poly2sym(polyfit(x,y,2))
```

p =

*3 * x ^ 2 + x + 2*

EXERCISE 6-6

Represent 200 points of cubic interpolation between the points (x, y) given by the values that the function takes exponential e ^ x using 20x values equally spaced between 0 and 2. Also represent the difference between the function e ^ x and its approximation by interpolation. Use cubic interpolation.

First, we define the 20 given points *(x, y)*, equally spaced between 0 and 2:

```
>> x = 0:0.1:2;
>> y = exp(x);
```

Now we find 200 points *(xi, yi)* for cubic interpolation, equally spaced between 0 and 2, and they are represented on a graph, together with the 20 points *(x, y)* using asterisks. See Figure 6-1:

```
>> xi = 0:0.01:2;
>> yi = interp1(x,y,xi,'cubic');
>> plot(x,y,'*',xi,yi)
```

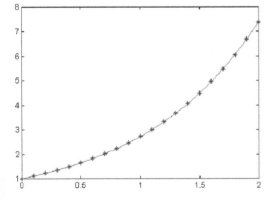

Figure 6-1.

131

It now represents the difference between the exact values of the graph of $y = e \wedge x$ in 200 interpolation points and its own points (x_i, y_i). So you have a graphic idea of the error committed by using interpolation points instead of the exact points. The error would be zero if the graph was reduced to the x axis. See Figure 6-2:

```
>> zi=(exp(xi));
>> di=yi-zi ;
>> plot(xi,di)
```

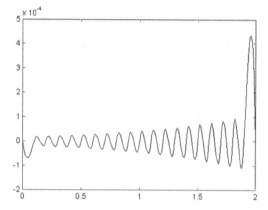

Figure 6-2.

EXERCISE 6-7

Get 25 points of approach by interpolation of the parametric function X = Cos(t), Y = Sin (t), Z = Tan(t) for values of *t* between 0 and π/6, on the set of points defined for values of t in the range $0 \leq t \leq 6$.

First, we define the 25 given points *(x, y, z)*, equally spaced between 0 and π /6.

```
>> t = 0: pi/150: pi/6;
>> x = cos(t); y = sin(t); z = tan(t);
```

Now find the 25 points of interpolation (x_i, y_i, z_i), for values of the parameter *t* equally spaced between 0 and π /6.

```
>> xi = cos(t); yi = sin(t);
>> zi = griddata(x,y,z,xi,yi);
>> points = [xi; yi; zi]'
```

points =

```
1.0000 0 0.0000
0.9998 0.0209 0.0161
0.9991 0.0419 0.0367
0.9980 0.0628 0.0598
0.9965 0.0837 0.0836
0.9945 0.1045 0.1057
```

```
0.9921 0.1253 0.1269
0.9893 0.1461 0.1480
0.9860 0.1668 0.1692
0.9823 0.1874 0.1907
0.9781 0.2079 0.2124
0.9736 0.2284 0.2344
0.9686 0.2487 0.2567
0.9632 0.2689 0.2792
0.9573 0.2890 0.3019
0.9511 0.3090 0.3249
0.9444 0.3289 0.3483
0.9373 0.3486 0.3719
0.9298 0.3681 0.3959
0.9219 0.3875 0.4203
0.9135 0.4067 0.4452
0.9048 0.4258 0.4706
0.8957 0.4446 0.4969
0.8862 0.4633 0.5236
0.8763 0.4818 0.5505
0.8660 0.5000 0.5774
```

EXERCISE 6-8

Get 30 points (xi, yi) for the periodic function y = Sin x for values of x that are equally spaced, interpolating them between 20 values of (x, y) given by y = sin (x) for x values evenly spaced in the interval (0, 2π), and using the interpolation method based on the fast Fourier transform (FFT).

First, we define the 20 *x* values equally spaced between 0 and 2π.

```
>> x = 0:pi/10:2*pi;
```

Now find the 30-point interpolation *(x, y)*.

```
>> y = interpft(sin(x), 30);
>> points = [y; asin(y)]'
```

points =

```
0.0000 0.0000
0.1878 0.1890
0.4499 0.4667
0.6070 0.6522
0.7614 0.8654
0.9042 1.1295
0.9618 1.2935
0.9963 1.4848
0.9913 1.4388
0.9106 1.1448
```

```
 0.8090  0.9425
 0.6678  0.7312
 0.4744  0.4943
 0.2813  0.2852
 0.0672  0.0673
-0.1640 - 0.1647
-0.3636 - 0.3722
-0.5597 - 0.5940
-0.7367 - 0.8282
-0.8538 - 1.0233
-0.9511 - 1.2566
-1.0035 - 1.5708 - 0. 0837i
-0.9818 - 1.3799
-0.9446 - 1.2365
-0.8526 - 1.0210
-0.6902 - 0.7617
-0.5484 - 0.5805
-0.3478 - 0.3553
-0.0807 - 0.0808
 0.0086  0.0086
```

EXERCISE 6-9

Find the polynomial of degree 3 which better adjusts the cloud of points for the pairs (i, i²) where $1 \le i \le 7$, in the least squares sense. Find your value for $x = 10$ and graphically represent the adjustment curve.

```
>> x=[1:7];y=[1,4,9,16,25,36,49];p=poly2sym(polyfit(x,y,2))
```

p =

x^2 - (5188368643045181*x)/63382530011411470074835160 2688 + 1315941209318717/7922816251426433 7593543950336

Now calculate the numerical value of the polynomial *p* for *x = 10*.

```
>> subs(p,10)
```

ans =

100

We can also approach the coefficients of the polynomial *p* to 5 digits.

>> **vpa(p,5)**

ans =

$x^2 - 0.000000000000081858*x + 0.00000000000001661$

Figure 6-3 represents the graph of adjustment:

>> **ezplot(p,[-5,5])**

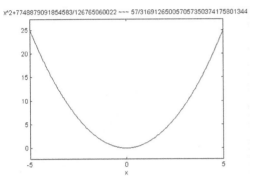

Figure 6-3.

■ ■ ■

Numbers, Variables, Operators and Functions Used in Graphics Programming

A.1 Variables

Variables and functions have an important role in graphical programming. Especially the vector and matrix variables. MATLAB does not require any command to declare variables. Simply create the variable by direct allocation of its value. For example:

```
>> v = 3

v =

    3
```

The variable v will be worth 3 unless its value is changed by using a new mapping. Once the variable is declared we can use it in calculations.

```
>> v ^ 3

Ans =

    27

>nmr4eb]\tb5r'> v+5

Ans =

    8
```

The value assigned to a variable is permanent, until changed explicitly it is defined outside the current MATLAB session.

If we now write:

`>> v = 3 + 7`

v =

    10

The variable v is worth 10 from now on, as shown in the following calculation:

`>> v ^ 4`

ans =

    10000

The variable names begin with a letter followed by any number of letters, digits or underscores, bearing in mind that MATLAB uses only the first 31 characters of the name of the variable. Also, it is very important point out that MATLAB is sensitive to capital letters and lowercase. Therefore, a variable with capital letters is different from the same variable with lowercase.

A.2 Numbers

You can work with different types of numbers and numerical expressions, which cover the entire field of numbers: integer, rational, real and complex numbers, and are used in arguments to functions in MATLAB.

Arithmetic operations in MATLAB are defined according to standard mathematical conventions. MATLAB is an interactive program that allows you to perform a variety of mathematical operations. MATLAB assumes the usual arithmetic operations of sum, difference, product, division and power, with the usual hierarchy between them:

x + y	*Sum*
x y	*Difference*
x * y or x y	*Product*
x/y	*Division*
x ^ y	*Power*

To add two numbers simply type the first number, type a plus sign (+) and the second number. It may include spaces before and after the sign so that the *input* is easier to read.

`>> 2 + 3`

Ans =

    5

We can perform the calculation of powers of a number as shown here.

```
>> 100 ^ 50
```

Ans =

  1.0000e + 100

Unlike a calculator, when working with integers, MATLAB displays the exact result even when you have more digits than would fit across the screen. MATLAB returns the exact value of *100 ^ 50* when using the vpa function discussed in detail later in this appendix.

```
>> vpa ' 99 ^ 50'
```

Ans =

  .60500606713753665044791996801256e100

To combine several operations into the same instruction you must take into account the usual criteria of priority among them that determine the order of evaluation of the expression. See the following example:

```
>> 2 * 3 ^ 2 + (5-2) * 3
```

Ans =

  27

Taking into account the priority of operators, the first to be evaluated is that of empowerment. The normal evaluation order can be altered by grouping expressions in parentheses.

In addition to these arithmetic operators, MATLAB is equipped with a set of basic functions and the user can also define their own functions. Both the leading embedded MATLAB functions and operators can be applied on symbolic constants or numbers.

MATLAB can be used for arithmetic operations as if it were a conventional calculator, but with one important difference: the precision in the calculation. Operations are performed as accurate, by specifying the user the degree of precision, as you want. This unlimited precision in the calculation is the feature which differs to other numerical calculation programs. MATLAB utilizes the word length that works for the computer to determine the accuracy, so it becomes something inherent to the hardware and cannot be modified.

The accuracy of the output of the results of operations with MATLAB can be relaxed using special techniques of approximation to the exact with a certain degree of precision in the result. MATLAB represents results with accuracy, but even if internally you always work with exact calculations to avoid rounding errors, you can enable different approximate representation formats, which sometimes facilitate the interpretation of results. The commands that allow numerical approximations are the following:

long format	*It delivers results with 16 decimals*
short format	*It offers results with 4 decimals. It's the default format of MATLAB*
format long e	*Provides the results to 16 decimal places where a power of 10 is required*
format short e	*Provides the results to four decimal places where the power of 10 is required*
format long g	*It offers results in optimal long format*
format short g	*It offers results in optimum short format*
bank format	*It delivers results with 2 decimals*
format rat	*It offers the results in the form of a rational number approximation*
format +	*Offers the results sign (+, -) and ignores the imaginary part of the complex numbers*
format hex	*It offers results in the hexadecimal system*
vpa 'operations' n	*It provides the result of operations with n exact decimal digits*
numeric ('expr')	*Provides the value of the expression as a numeric approximation in the active current format*
digits (n)	*It offers the results with n digits*

Using *format* gives a numerical approximation of 174/13 in the way specified in the format:

```
>> 174/13
```

years =

        13.3846

```
>> long format; 174/13
```

years =

        13.38461538461539

```
>> format long e; 174/13
```

years =

        1.338461538461539e + 001

```
>> format short e; 174/13
```

years =

        1.3385e + 001

```
>> format long g; 174/13
```

years =

        13.3846153846154

```
>> format short g; 174/13
```

years =

        13.385

```
>> format bank; 174/13
```

years =

        13.38

```
>> format hex; 174/13
```

years =

        402ac4ec4ec4ec4f

Now we will see examples of the calculation of the value of the *sqrt (17)* with the number of decimal places and precision that we desire:

```
>> vpa ' 174/13 ' 10
```

years =

        13.38461538

```
>> vpa ' 174/13 ' 15
```

years =

        13.3846153846154

```
>> digits (20); VPA ' 174/13 '
```

years =

        13.384615384615384615

A.3 Integer Numbers

In MATLAB all common operations with integer numbers are accurately, regardless of the size of the output of the result. If we want the result of an operation to appear on screen with a certain number of exact figures, we use the command of symbolic computation ***vpa*** (*variable precision arithmetic*), whose syntax we already know.

For example, 6 to the power of 400 with 450 exact numbers is obtained as follows:

```
>> ' 6 vpa ^ 400' 450
```

Ans =

18217977168218728251394687124089371267338971528174760667459697549333959972090532700302826780076628386733147959945591636745242157445605964680105495406215017704234999886990788594743994796171248406730973807365248505631155692085087859428300809999273107625073394840473935055193456574397967882415119723262994774858 1376.

The result of the operation is accurate, always bring up a point at the end of the result. In this case, it was not necessary to use 450 figures to express the result of the proposed operation. If you require a smaller number of exact figures that actually would generate the exact result, MATLAB calculates the number requested and rounds the result and presents it including powers of 10. For example, we will perform the above calculation only with only 50 exact figures.

```
>> ' 6 vpa ^ 400' 50
```

Ans =

.18217977168218728251394687124089371267338971528175e312

A.4 Functions with Integer Numbers and Divisibility

There are several functions in MATLAB with integer arguments, the majority of which are related to divisibility. Among the most typical functions with integer arguments are the following:

rem (n, m)	*Remainder of the division of n and m (valid function for n and m real)*
sign (n)	*Sign of n (1 if n > 0, - 1 if n < 0, true)*
max (n1, n2)	*Maximum of n1 and n2 numbers*
min (n1, n2)	*Minimum of n1 and n2 numbers*
gcd (n1, n2)	*Greatest common divisor of n1 and n2*
lcm (n1, n2)	*Least common multiple of n1 and n2*
factorial (n)	*N factorial (n(n-1) (n-2)...)1)*
factor (n)	*It decomposes the n factorization*

Below are some examples.
Remainder of the division of 17 by 3:

```
>> rem (17.3)
```

Ans =

2

Remainder of division of 4.1 by 1.2:

```
>> rem (4.1,1.2)
```

Ans =

    0.5000

The remainder of the division of -4.1 and 1.2:

```
>> rem (-4.1, 1.2)
```

Ans =

    -0.5000

Maximum common divisor of 1,000, 500 and 625:

```
>> gcd (1000, gcd (500,625))
```

Ans =

    125.00

The least common multiple of 1,000, 500 and 625:

```
>> lcm (1000, lcm (500,625))
```

Ans =

    5000.00

A.5 Numbering Systems

MATLAB allows you to work with any base numbering systems, as long as the extended symbolic math *Toolbox* is available. It also allows to express all kinds of numbers in different bases. This implements the following functions:

dec2base (decimal, n_base)	*Converts a decimal (base 10) number specified to the new base given by n_base*
base2dec(number,B)	*Converts the given base B number to a decimal number*
dec2bin (decimal)	*Converts the specified base 2 (binary) number to a decimal number*
dec2hex (decimal)	*Converts the specified base 16 (hexadecimal) to a decimal number*
bin2dec (binary)	*Convert the binary number to a decimal base*
hex2dec (hexadecimal)	*It converts the number base 16 specified to a decimal base*

Below are some examples.
Represent the base 2 number 100101 in base 10.

```
>> base2dec('100101',2)
```

Ans =

   37.00

Represent the hexadecimal number FFFFAA00 in base 10.

```
>> base2dec ('FFFFAA0', 16)
```

Ans =

   268434080.00

Calculate the result in base 10 of the operation FFFAA2 + FF – 1

```
>> base2dec('FFFAA2',16) + base2dec('FF',16)-1
```

years =

   16776096.00

A.6 Real Numbers

A rational number is of the form p/q, where p is an integer and q another integer. The way in which the rational is different in MATLAB from that of the majority of calculators is that the integer forms are retained through calculations. If we ask a calculator to calculate the sum $1/2 + 1/3 + 1/4$, most will return something like *1.0833*, which is no more than an approximation to the result.

MATLAB can work with rational numbers in exact mode, so the result of expressions involving rational numbers is always another rational or whole number. If so, it is necessary to activate this format with the command *format rat*. But MATLAB also returns approaches using decimals in the results if the user so wishes, by activating any other type of format (e.g. *format short* or *format long*). MATLAB solves the calculator operation above in exact mode in the following way:

```
>> format rat
>> 1/2 + 1/3 + 1/4
```

Ans =

   13/12

Unlike calculators, to make operations with rational numbers the result always can be accurate. Therefore, while MATLAB is dealing with rationals as ratios of integers, it keeps them in this way. In this way, rounding errors are not dragged in calculations with fractions, which can become very serious, as evidenced by the theory of errors. Note that, once enabled in rational format, when calling MATLAB that you add two rationals, it returns a rational as a ratio of integers and thus represent it symbolically. Once enabled in the rational format, operations with rationals will be exact until changed to a different format.

A number in floating point, or a number with a decimal point, is interpreted as exact if rational format is enabled. If there is a number with a floating point expression, MATLAB is entirely exact in how the rational expression is represented with the result in rational numbers.

```
>> format rat
>> 10/23 + 2.45/44
```

Ans =

    1183 / 2412

The other fundamental subset within the actual numbers is irrational numbers, which have always created difficulties in the processes of numerical calculations by their special nature. The impossibility of representing an irrational accurately in numeric mode (using the ten digits from the decimal numbering system) is the cause of most of the problems. MATLAB represents the results with greater accuracy which can be the accuracy required by the user. The irrational cannot be represented exactly as the ratio of two integers. If you try the square root of the number 17, MATLAB returns the number 5.1962 in that format by default.

```
>> sqrt (27)
```

Ans =

    5.1962

There is a large group of irrational and real numbers deserving special treatment for common use. MATLAB incorporates the following:

pi	*Number $\pi = 3.1415926$*
exp (1)	*Number $e = 2.7182818$*
inf	*Infinity (for example 1/0)*
nan	*Uncertainty (for example 0/0)*
realmin	*Least usable positive real number*
realmax	*Greatest usable positive real number*

Then these numbers with outputs of MATLAB are illustrated as follows:

```
>> long format
>> pi
```

years =

    3.14159265358979

```
>> exp (1)
```

Ans =

    2.71828182845905

>> **1/0**

Warning: Divide by zero.

ans =

   Inf

>> **0/0**

Warning: Divide by zero.

Ans =

   NaN

>> **realmin**

Ans =

   2. 225073858507201e-308

>> **realmax**

Ans =

   1. 797693134862316e + 308

A.7 Functions with Real Arguments

The disjoint union of the set of rational numbers and the set of irrational numbers is the set of real numbers. In turn, the set of rational numbers contains the set of integers. All functions applicable to real numbers will be valid also for integer, rational and irrational numbers. MATLAB provides a full range of predefined functions, some of which are discussed in chapters of this book. Within the group of functions with real arguments offered by MATLAB, the most important are the following:

Trigonometric functions

Function	Reverse
sin (x)	asin (x)
cos (x)	acos (x)
tan(x)	atan(x) atan2 (x)
csc (x)	acsc (x)
sec (x)	asec (x)
cot (x)	acot (x)

Hyperbolic functions

Function	Reverse
sinh (x)	asinh (x)
cosh (x)	acosh (x)
tanh (x)	atanh (x)
csch (x)	acsch (x)
sech (x)	asech (x)
coth (x)	acoth (x)

Exponential and logarithmic functions

Function	Meaning
exp (x)	*Exponential function in base e (e ^ x)*
log (x)	*Function for the logarithm base e of x*
log10 (x)	*The logarithm base 10 of x*
log2 (x)	*The logarithm base 2 of x*
pow2 (x)	*Power function-base 2 of x*
sqrt (x)	*Square root of x*

Numeric variable-specific functions

Function	Meaning
abs (x)	*Absolute value of the real x*
floor (x)	*The largest integer less than or equal to the real x*
ceil (x)	*The smallest integer greater than or equal to the real x*
round (x)	*The closest integer to the real x*
fix (x)	*Eliminates the decimal part of the real x*
rem (a, b)	*It gives the remainder of the division between the real a and b*
sign (x)	*Sign of the real x (1 if x > 0, - 1 if x < 0)*

Here are some examples:

```
>> sin(pi/2)
```

Ans =

    1

>> **asin (1)**

years =

    1.57079632679490

>> **log (exp (1) ^ 3)**

years =

    3.00000000000000

The meaning of the function *round* is illustrated in the following two cases:

>> **round (2.574)**

years =

    3

>> **round (2.4)**

years =

    2

The meaning of the function *ceil* is illustrated in the following two cases:

>> **ceil (4.2)**

years =

    5

>> **ceil (4.8)**

years =

    5

The meaning of the function *floor* we see in the following two examples:

>> **floor (4.2)**

years =

    4

`>> floor (4.8)`

years =

    4

Fix function is limited to removing the decimal part of a real number:

`>> fix (5.789)`

Ans =

    5

A.8 Random Numbers

MATLAB automatically generates random numbers. It provides the function *rand* to generate uniformly distributed random numbers and the function *randn* to generate normally distributed random numbers. The most interesting features of MATLAB generated random numbers are presented in the following table:

rand	*Returns a decimal random number uniformly distributed on the interval [0,1]*
rand (n)	*Returns an array of size n x n whose elements are uniformly distributed random decimal numbers in the interval [0,1]*
rand (m, n)	*Returns an array of dimension m x n whose elements are uniformly distributed random decimal numbers in the interval [0,1]*
rand (size (a))	*Returns an array of the same size as the matrix A and whose elements are uniformly distributed random decimal numbers in the interval [0,1]*
rand ('seed')	*Returns the current value of the uniform random number generator seed*
rand('seed',n)	*Placed at the number n, the current value of the uniform random number generator seed*
randn	*Returns a normally distributed random decimal number according to a mean of 0 and variance 1*
randn (n)	*Returns an array of size n x n whose elements are normally distributed random decimal numbers according to a mean of 0 and variance 1*
randn (m, n)	*Returns an array of dimension mxn whose elements are normally distributed random decimal numbers according to a mean 0 and variance 1*
randn (size (a))	*Returns an array of random decimal numbers the same size as the matrix A and whose elements are normally distributed according to a mean of 0 and variance 1*
randn ('seed')	*Returns the current value of the normal random number generator seed*
randn('seed',n)	*Placed in the n number, the current value of the uniform random number generator seed*

Here are some examples:

```
>> [rand, rand(1), randn, randn(1)]
```

ans =

```
    0.9501     0.2311    -0.4326    -1.6656
```

```
>> [rand(2), randn(2)]
```

ans =

```
    0.6068     0.8913              0.1253    -1.1465
    0.4860     0.7621              0.2877     1.1909
```

```
>> [rand(2,3), randn(2,3)]
```

years =

```
    0.3529 0.0099 0.2028         -0.1364 1.0668-0.0956
    0.8132    389 0.1987          0.1139 0.0593-0.8323
```

A.9 Complex Numbers

Work in the field of complex numbers is implemented in MATLAB. MATLAB of course follows the convention of using an *i* or a *j* to represent the *imaginary number* $\sqrt{-1}$, which is the key value in all the analysis of complex variables. Over the complex numbers can be applied the usual operators, as well as some specific functions. Both the real part and the imaginary part of the complex numbers can be any real number or symbolic constants, and operations with them, which are in exact mode, unless involved in any closer decimal, in which case it returns an approximation of the result. As the imaginary unit is represented by the symbols *i* or *j*, the complex numbers are expressed in the form *a+bi* or *a+bj*. It is worth noting the fact that don't need the product (the asterisk) symbol before the imaginary unit:

```
>> (1-5i)*(1-i)/(-1+2i)
```

ans =

```
    -1.6000 + 2.8000i
```

```
>> format rat
>> (1-5i)*(1-i)/(-1+2i)
```

Ans =

```
    -8/5 + 14/5i
```

A.10 Functions with Complex Arguments

Working with complex variables is very important in mathematical analysis and their applications in major branches of engineering. MATLAB implements not only the possibility of operating with complex numbers, but it also incorporates various functions for complex variables. Below is a summary of the most important.

Trigonometric functions

Function	Reverse
sin (z)	asin (z)
cos (z)	acos (z)
tan(z)	atan(z) atan2 (z)
sec (z)	asec (z)
csc (z)	acsc (z)
cot (z)	acot (z)

Hyperbolic functions

Function	Reverse
sinh (z)	asinh (z)
cosh(z)	acosh(z)
tanh(z)	atanh(z)
csch(z)	acsch(z)
sech(z)	asech(z)
coth (z)	acoth (z)

Exponential and logarithmic functions

Function	Meaning
exp (Z)	*Exponential function in base e (e ^ Z)*
log (Z)	*Logarithm base e of Z*
log10 (Z)	*Logarithm base 10 of Z*
log2 (Z)	*Logarithm base 2 of Z*
pow2 (Z)	*Power function-based 2 of Z*
sqrt (Z)	*Square root of Z*

Specific functions for the real and imaginary part

Function	Meaning
floor (Z)	*Applies the floor function to (Z) for real and imag (Z)*
ceil (Z)	*Applies the ceil function to (Z) for real and imag (Z)*
round (Z)	*Applies the function round (Z) for real and imag (Z)*
fix (Z)	*Applies the function fix (Z) for real and imag (Z)*

Specific functions for the real and imaginary part

Function	Meaning
abs (Z)	*Module of the complex Z*
angle (Z)	*Argument of the complex Z*
conj (Z)	*Complex conjugate of Z*
real (Z)	*Real part of the complex Z*
imag (Z)	*Imaginary part of the complex Z*

Below are some examples of operations with complex numbers.

`>> round(1.5-3.4i)`

ans =

   2   -   3*i*

`>> real(i^i)`

ans =

   0.2079

`>> (2+2i)^2/(-3-3*sqrt(3)*i)^90`

Ans =

   0502e-085 - 1 + 7. 4042e-070*i*

`>> sin(1+i)`

Ans =

   1.2985. 6350*i*

A.11 Operators

MATLAB has operators to perform calculations involving arithmetic, logical, relational, and conditional operations.

A.11.1 Arithmetic Operators

There are two types of arithmetic operations in MATLAB: matrix arithmetic operations, which are governed by the rules of linear algebra, and arithmetic operations with vectors, which are performed element to element. The operators involved are presented in the following table.

Operator	Role Played
+	*Sum of scalar, vector, or matrix*
-	*Subtraction of scalar, vector, or matrix*
*	*Product of scalar or array*
.*	*Product of scalar or vector*
\	$A\backslash B = inv(A) * B$, *with A and B being matrices*
.\	$A.\backslash B = [B(i,j)/A(i,j)]$, *with A and B being vectors [dim (A) = dim (B)]*
/	$b/a = B * inv(A)$, *with A and B being matrices*
./	$A/B = [A(i,j)/b(i,j)]$, *with A and B being vectors [dim (A) = dim (B)]*
^	*Power of a scalar or power of the matrix (M p)*
.^	*Power of vectors (a.$^\wedge$ B = [A(i,j)B (i, j)], for vectors A and B)*

Simple mathematical operations between scalars and vectors apply scale to all elements of the vector according to the defined operation, and simple operations between vectors are performed element to element. Below is a specification of these operators:

a = {a1, a2,..., an}, b = {b1, b2,..., bn} c = scale	
a + c = [a1 + c a2 + c ... an+c]	*Sum of a scalar and a vector*
a * c = [a1 * c a2 * c ... an * c]	*Product of a scalar by a vector*
a + b = [a1+b1 a2+b2 ... an+bn]	*Sum of two vectors*
a. * b = [a1*b1 a2*b2 ... an*bn]	*Product of two vectors*
a. / b = [a1/b1 a2/b2 ... an/bn]	*Ratio of two vectors to the right*
a. \ b = [a1\b1 a2\b2 ... an\bn]	*Ratio to the left of two vectors*
a. ^ c = [a1 ^c a2 ^ c... an ^ c]	*Vector to a power*
c. ^ a = [c ^ a1 c ^ a2 ... c ^ an]	*c to the a vector*
a.^b = [a1^b1 a2^b2 ... an^bn]	*Vector to a vector power*

It must be borne in mind that the vectors must be of the same length and that for the product, quotient, and power, the first operand is followed by a point (dot).

The following is an example that involves this type of operators.

```
>> X = [5,4,3]; Y = [1,2,7]; a = X + Y, b = X-Y, c = x * Y, d = 2. * X,...
e = 2/X, f = 2. \Y, g = x / Y, h =. \X, i = x ^ 2, j = 2. ^ X, k = X. ^ y

A =

    6 6 10

b =

    -4 2-4
```

$c =$

   5 8 21

$d =$

   10 8 6

$e =$

   0.4000 0.5000 0.6667

$f =$

   0.5000 1.0000 3.5000

$g =$

   5.0000 2.0000 0.4286

$h =$

   5.0000 2.0000 0.4286

$i =$

   25 16 9

$j =$

   32 16 8

$k =$

   5 16 2187

Since the variable operands are vectors of the same dimension in all cases, the operations will be carried out element to element (for the sum and the difference there is no distinction between vectors and matrices, as they are identical operations in both cases).

In terms of operators with array variables, the most important are specified below:

A + B, A-B, A * B	*Addition, subtraction and the product of matrices*
A\B	*If A is square, A\B = inv (A) * B. If A is not square, A\B is the solution in the sense of least-squares system AX = B*
B/A	*Coincides with (A ' \ B')'*
Aⁿ	*Matches A * A * A *... * N times (n scale)*
pᴬ	*Performs the calculation only if p is a scalar*

Here are some examples:

```
>> X = [5,4,3]; Y = [1,2,7]; l = X'* Y, m = X * Y ', n = 2 * X, o = X / Y, p = Y\X
```

l =

```
    5 10 35
    4  8 28
    3  6 21
```

m =

```
    34
```

n =

```
    10 8 6
```

o =

```
    0.6296
```

p =

```
    0          0          0
    0          0          0
    0.7143     0.5714     0.4286
```

All previous operations are defined in matrix form with the proper dimension. We must not forget that a vector is a particular case of a matrix, but to operate with it in matrix form (not element by element), it is necessary to respect the rules of dimensionality for matrix operations. Vector operations $x. ' * Y$ and $X.*Y'$ make no sense, since different dimensions of vectors are operating. Matrix operations $X * Y$, $2/X$, $2\backslash Y$, $X \wedge 2$, $2 \wedge X$ and $X \wedge Y$ make no sense, since there are errors of dimensionality committed in the arrays.

Here are more examples of matrix operators.

```
>> M = [1,2,3;1,0,2;7,8,9]
```

M =

```
    1 2 3
    1 0 2
    7 8 9
```

```
>> B = inv (M), C = M ^ 2, D = M ^(1/2), E = 2 ^ M
```

B =

```
    -0.8889     0.3333     0.2222
     0.2778 -  0.6667     0.0556
     0.4444     0.3333 -  0.1111
```

$C =$

24	26	34
15	18	21
78	86	118

$D =$

$0.5219 + 0.8432i$	$0.5793 - 0.0664i$	$0.7756 - 0.2344i$
$0.3270 + 0.0207i$	$0.3630 + 1.0650i$	$0.4859 - 0.2012i$
$1.7848 - 0.5828i$	$1.9811 - 0.7508i$	$2.6524 + 0.3080i$

$E =$

$1.0e + 003 *$

0.8626	0.9568	1.2811
0.5401	0.5999	0.8027
2.9482	725	4.3816

A.11.2 Relational Operators

MATLAB also provides symbols to denote the relational operations. Relational operators perform comparisons element by element between two matrices and return an array of the same size whose elements are zero if the corresponding relationship is true, or one if the corresponding relation is false. The relational operators can also compare scalar vectors or matrices, in which case it is compared with all the elements of the array. Below is a table with these operators.

<	*Less than (for complex, affects only real parts)*
< =	*Less than or equal (only applies to real parts)*
>	*Greater than (only applies to real parts)*
> =	*Greater than or equal (only applies to real parts)*
x == y	*Equality (affects complex numbers)*
x ~ = y	*Inequality (affects complex numbers)*

A.11.3 Logical Operators

MATLAB provides symbols to denote logical operations. The logical operators offer a way to combine or deny relational expressions. The following table shows this type of operator:

~ A	*Logical negation (NOT) or A supplementary*
A & B	*Logical conjunction (AND) or intersection of A and B*
A | B	*Logical disjunction (OR) or union of A and B*
XOR (A, B)	*OR exclusive (XOR) or symmetric difference of A and B (worth 1 if A or B, but not both)*

Here are some examples:

```
>> A = 2:7;P =(A>3) & (A<6)
```

```
P =

    0    0    1    1    0    0
```

Returns 1 when A is greater than 3 and less than 6, and returns 0 otherwise.

```
>> X = 3 * ones (3.3); X > = [7 8 9; 4 5 6 and 1 2 3]
```

```
Ans =
    0 0 0
    0 0 0
    1 1 1
```

The elements of the array X which are greater or equal to that of the matrix *[7 8 9; 4 5 6 and 1 2 3]* correspond to a 1 in the matrix response. The rest of the elements correspond to a 0.

A.12.4 Logical Functions

MATLAB implements logical functions whose output is of the true type (value 1) or false (value 0). The following table shows the most important:

exist (A)	*Checks if the variable or function exists (returns 0 if A does not exist and a number between 1 and 5, depending on the type, if it exists)*
any (V)	*Returns 0 if all elements of the vector V are null and returns 1 if some element of V are non-zero*
any(A)	*Returns 0 for each column of the matrix A with all null elements and returns 1 for each column of the matrix A with some of its elements non-null*
all (V)	*Returns 1 if all the elements of the vector V are non-null and returns 0 if some element of V is null*
all(A)	*Returns 1 for each column of the matrix A with all the non-null elements and returns 0 for each column of the matrix A with some of its elements void*
find (V)	*Returns the places (or indices) that occupy the non-null elements of the vector V*
isnan (V)	*Returns 1 for the elements of V that are indeterminate and returns 0 for those that are not*
isinf (V)	*Returns 1 for the elements of V that are infinite and returns 0 for those that are not*
isfinite (V)	*Returns 1 for the elements of V that are finite and returns 0 for those that are not*
Isempty (A)	*Returns 1 if A is an empty array and returns 0 otherwise (an empty array has one of its dimensions 0)*
issparse (A)	*Returns 1 if A is an array of boxes and returns 0 otherwise*
Isreal (V)	*It returns 1 if all the elements of V are real and 0 otherwise*
isprime (V)	*Returns 1 for all elements of V that are prime and returns 0 for elements of V that are not prime*
islogical (V)	*It returns 1 if V is a logical vector and 0 otherwise*

(continued)

isnumeric (V)	*It returns 1 if V is a numeric vector and 0 otherwise*
ishold	*It returns 1 if they retain the properties of the current graph for the next and for those only added new and otherwise 0*
isieee	*Returns 1 for IEEE computer*
isstr (S)	*It returns 1 if S is a string and 0 otherwise*
ischart (S)	*It returns 1 if S is a string and 0 otherwise*
IsGlobal (A)	*Returns 1 if A is a global variable and 0 otherwise*
IsLetter (S)	*It returns 1 if S is a letter of the alphabet and 0 otherwise*
IsEqual (A, B)	*Returns 1 if the matrices or vectors A and B are equal, and 0 otherwise*
IsMember (V, W)	*Returns 1 for every element of V which is in W and 0 for every element V that is not in W*

Below are some examples of logical functions in use.

```
>> V=[1,2,3,4,5,6,7,8,9], isprime(V), isnumeric(V), all(V), any(V)
```

V =

   1   2   3   4   5   6   7   8   9

years =

   0   1   1   0   1   0   1   0   0

years =

   1

years =

   1

years =

   1

```
>> B=[Inf, -Inf, pi, NaN], isinf(B), isfinite(B), isnan(B), isreal(B)
```

B =

   INF - Inf 3.1416 NaN

years =

   1 1 0 0

years =

     0 0 1 0

years =

     0 0 0 1

years =

     1

>> **ismember ([1,2,3], [8,12,1,3]), A = [2,0,1];B = [4,0,2]; isequal (2A * B)**

Ans =

     1 0 1

Ans =

     1

A.12 Vector Variables

A vector variable of n elements can be defined in MATLAB in the following ways:

V = [v1, v2, v3,..., vn]

V = [v1 v2 v3... vn]

When you apply most commands and functions of MATLAB on a vector variable the result obtained is the application of the command or function on each element of the vector:

>> **vector1 = [1,4,9,2.25,1/4]**

vector1 =

     1.0000 4.0000 9.0000 2.2500 0.2500

>> **sqrt (vector1)**

Ans =

     1.0000 2.0000 3.0000 1.5000 0.5000

There are different ways of defining a vector variable without explicitly bracketing all its elements separated by commas or blank spaces. They are presented in the following table:

variable = [a: b]	*Defines the vector whose first and last elements are a and b, respectively, and the intermediate elements differ in one unit*
variable = [a: s:b]	*Defines the vector whose first and last elements are a and b, and the intermediate elements differ in the amount specified by the increase in s*
variable = linespace [a, b, n]	*Defines the vector whose first and last elements are a and b, and has in total n evenly spaced elements*
variable = logspace [a, b, n]	*It defines the vector whose first and last elements are specified and has in total n evenly spaced elements together on a logarithmic scale*

Below are some examples:

>> vector2 = [5:5:25]

Vector2 =

5 10 15 20 25

We have retrieved the numbers between 5 and 25 separated by 5 units.

>> vector3 = [10:30]

Vector3 =

Columns 1 through 13

10 11 12 13 14 15 16 17 18 19 20 21 22

Columns 14 through 21

23 24 25 26 27 28 29 30

We have obtained the numbers between 10 and 30 including the endpoints.

>> t:Microsoft.WindowsMobile.DirectX.Vector4 = linspace (10,30,6)

t:Microsoft.WindowsMobile.DirectX.Vector4 =

10 14 18 22 26 30

We have obtained 6 numbers between 10 and 30 inclusive, equally spaced.

```
>> vector5 = logspace (10,30,6)
```

vector5 =

   *1. 0e + 030 ***

   0.0000 0.0000 0.0000 0.0000 0.0001 1.0000

We have obtained 6 numbers between antilogarithm decimal of 0 and antilogarithm decimal of 2, spaced evenly.

There is also the possibility of considering vector row and column vectors in MATLAB. A column vector is obtained by separating its elements by semicolons, or also transposing a vector row using a single quotation mark located at the end of its definition.

```
>> a=[10;20;30;40]
```

a =

   10
   20
   30
   40

```
>> a=(10:14);b=a'
```

b =

   10
   11
   12
   13
   14

```
>> c=(a')'
```

c =

   10   11   12   13   14

You can also select an element of a vector or a subset of elements. The following table shows the rules:

x (n)	*Returns the nth element of the vector x*
x(a:b)	*Returns the elements of the vector x between the a-th and the b-th, both inclusive*
x(a:p:b)	*Returns the elements of the vector x located between the a-th and the b-th, both inclusive, but separated by p units (a > b).*
x(b:-p:a)	*Returns the elements of the vector x located between the b-th and a-th, both inclusive, but separated by p units and starting with the b-th (b > a)*

Here are some examples:

```
>> x =(1:10)
```

X =

```
   1    2    3    4    5    6    7    8    9    10
```

```
>> x (6)
```

Ans =

```
   6
```

We have obtained the sixth element of the vector x.

```
>> x(4:7)
```

Ans =

```
   4 5 6 7
```

We have obtained the elements of the vector x located between the fourth and the seventh, both inclusive.

```
>> x(2:3:9)
```

Ans =

```
   2-5-8
```

We have obtained the elements of the vector x located between the second and ninth, both inclusive, but separated by three units. Note the 9 does not conform the the rule and so is not included in the answer.

```
>> x(9:-3:2)
```

Ans =

```
   9 6 3
```

We have obtained the elements of the vector x located between the ninth and second, both inclusive, but separated in three units and starting at the ninth.

A.13 Matrix Variables

MATLAB defines arrays by inserting brackets around all its row vectors separated by a comma. Vectors can be entered by separating its components by whitespace or comma, as we already know. For example, a dimension 3 x 3 matrix variable can be entered in the following two ways:

$\mathbf{M} = [\mathbf{a}_{11}\ \mathbf{a}_{12}\ \mathbf{a}_{13};\ \mathbf{a}_{21}\ \mathbf{a}_{22}\ \mathbf{a}_{23};\ \mathbf{a}_{31}\ \mathbf{a}_{32}\ \mathbf{a}_{33}]$

$\mathbf{M} = [\mathbf{a}_{11},\ \mathbf{a}_{12},\ \mathbf{a}_{13};\ \mathbf{a}_{21},\ \mathbf{a}_{22},\ \mathbf{a}_{23};\ \mathbf{a}_{31},\ \mathbf{a}_{32},\ \mathbf{a}_{33}]$

It would define an array variable of dimension *(M x N)* similarly. Once a matrix variable has been defined, MATLAB enables many options to insert, extract, renumber, and generally manipulate its elements. The following table shows different possibilities of definition of matrix variables.

A(m,n)	*Defines the (m, n) element of the matrix A (row m and column n)*
A(a:b,c:d)	*Defines the subarray of A formed by rows between the a-th and the b-th and the columns between the c-th and the d-th*
A(a:p:b,c:q:d)	*Defines the subarray of A formed by the rows between the a-th and the b-th spaced by p in p, and the columns between the c-th and the d-th spaced by q in q*
A([a b],[c d])	*Defines the subarray of A formed by the intersection of the rows a-th and the b-th and columns c-th and the d-th*
A([a b c...],) ([e f g...])	*Defines the subarray of A formed by the intersection of rows a, b, c,... and columns e, f, g,...*
A(:,c:d)	*Defines the subarray of A formed by all the rows from A and columns between the c-th and the d-th*
A(:,[c d e...])	*Defines the subarray of A formed by all the rows from A and columns c, d, e,...*
A(a:b,:)	*Defines the subarray of A formed by all the columns in A and rows between the a-th and the b-th*
A([a b c...],:)	*Defines the subarray of A formed by all the columns in A and rows a, b, c,...*
A(a,:)	*Defines the a-th row of the matrix A*
A(:,b)	*Defines the b-th column of the matrix A*
A (:)	*Defines a vector column whose elements are the columns of A placed one below another*
A(:,:)	*It is equivalent to all of the matrix A*
[A, B, C,...]	*Defines the matrix formed by the XCF of A, B, C,...*
SA = [ ]	*Clears the subarray of the matrix A, SA , and returns the remainder*
diag (v)	*Creates a diagonal matrix with the vector v in the diagonal*
diag (A)	*Extracts the diagonal of the matrix as a vector column*
eye (n)	*It creates the identity matrix of order n*
eye (m, n)	*Creates and order m x n matrix with ones on the main diagonal and zeros elsewhere*
zeros (m, n)	*Creates the zero matrix of order m x n*
ones (m, n)	*Creates the matrix of order m x n with all its elements 1*
rand (m, n)	*It creates a uniform random matrix of order m x n*
randn (m, n)	*Creates a normal random matrix of order m x n*
flipud (A)	*Returns the matrix whose rows are placed in reverse order (from top to bottom) of the rows of A*
fliplr (A)	*Returns the matrix whose columns are placed in reverse (from left to right) of the columns of a*

(continued)

rot90 (A)	*Rotates the matrix A 90 degrees*
reshape(A,m,n)	*Returns the array of order m x n extracted from matrix A taking consecutive items by columns*
size (A)	*Returns the order (size) of the matrix A*
find (Acond)	*Returns items of A that meet a condition*
length (v)	*Returns the length of the vector v*
tril (A)	*Returns the lower triangular part of matrix A*
triu (A)	*Returns the upper triangular part of matrix A*
A'	*Returns the transpose of matrix A*
inv (A)	*Returns the inverse of matrix A*

Here are some examples:

We consider first the *2 x 3* matrix whose rows are the 6 consecutive odd first:

```
>> A = [1 3 5; 7-9-11]
```

TO =

```
1-3-5
7-9-11
```

Now we are going to cancel the element *(2,3)*, that is, its last element:

```
>> A(2,3) = 0
```

TO =

```
1-3-5
7 9 0
```

Then consider the matrix *B* that is the transpose of *A*:

```
>> B = A'
```

B =

```
1 7
3 9
5 0
```

We now construct a matrix *C*, formed by the matrix *B* and the matrix identity of order 3 attached to its right:

```
>> C = [B eye (3)]
```

C =

```
1   7   1   0   0
3   9   0   1   0
5   0   0   0   1
```

We are going to build a matrix *D* extracting odd columns of the matrix *C*, a parent *and* formed by the intersection of the first two rows of *C* and its third and fifth columns, and a matrix *F* formed by the intersection of the first two rows and the last three columns of the matrix *C*:

```
>> D = C(:,1:2:5)
```

D =

```
1 1 0
3 0 0
5-0-1
```

```
>> E = C([1 2],[3 5])
```

E =

```
1 0
0 0
```

```
>> F = C([1 2],3:5)
```

F =

```
1 0 0
0 1 0
```

Now we build the diagonal matrix *G* such that the elements of the main diagonal are the same as those of the main diagonal of *D*:

```
>> G = diag (diag (D))
```

G =

```
1 0 0
0 0 0
0 0 1
```

Then build the matrix H, formed by the intersection of the first and third rows of C and its second, third and fifth columns:

```
>> H = C([1 3],[2 3 5])
```

H =

```
    7 1 0
    0 0 1
```

Now we build an array I formed by the identity matrix of order 5×4 and zero matrices of the same order attached to the right. Then we extract the first row of I and, finally, form the matrix J with the odd rows and the pairs *and* columns and calculate the order (size).

```
>> I = [eye (5.4) zeros (5.4) ones (5.4)]
```

Ans =

```
    1    0    0    0    0    0    0    0    1    1    1    1
    0    1    0    0    0    0    0    0    1    1    1    1
    0    0    1    0    0    0    0    0    1    1    1    1
    0    0    0    1    0    0    0    0    1    1    1    1
    0    0    0    0    0    0    0    0    1    1    1    1
```

```
>> I(1,:)
```

ans =

```
    1    0    0    0    0    0    0    0    1    1    1    1
```

```
>> J = I (1:2:5, 2:2:12)
```

J =

```
    0    0    0    0    1    1
    0    0    0    0    1    1
    0    0    0    0    1    1
```

```
>> size (J)
```

ans =

```
    3    6
```

We then construct a random K matrix of order 3×4 and invert first in order of their rows, then by the order of the columns and then the order of the rows and columns at once. Finally, we find the matrix L of order 4×3 whose columns are taking the elements of $K's$ columns sequentially.

```
>> K = rand (3,4)
```

K =

```
    0.5269    0.4160    0.7622    0.7361
    0.0920    0.7012    0.2625    0.3282
    0.6539    0.9103    0.0475    0.6326
```

`>> K(3:-1:1,:)`

ans =

0.6539	0.9103	0.0475	0.6326
0.0920	0.7012	0.2625	0.3282
0.5269	0.4160	0.7622	0.7361

`>> K(:,4:-1:1)`

ans =

0.7361	0.7622	0.4160	0.5269
0.3282	0.2625	0.7012	0.0920
0.6326	0.0475	0.9103	0.6539

`>> K(3:-1:1,4:-1:1)`

ans =

0.6326	0.0475	0.9103	0.6539
0.3282	0.2625	0.7012	0.0920
0.7361	0.7622	0.4160	0.5269

`>> L = reshape(K, 4, 3)`

L =

0.5269	0.7012	0.0475
0.0920	0.9103	0.7361
0.6539	0.7622	0.3282
0.4160	0.2625	0.6326

A.14 Elementary Functions that Support Complex Vectors

MATLAB is software which handles vector and matrix calculations. Its name, *matrix laboratory*, already gives an idea of its power to work with vectors and matrices. MATLAB allows you to work with functions of a complex variable, but in addition this variable can be even matrix and vector. Below is a table with the functions of complex variable vectors that are incorporated in MATLAB.

max (v)	*Maximum component (max is calculated for complex (abs (V)))*
min (v)	*Minimum component (min is calculated for complex (abs (V)))*
mean (v)	*Average of the components of V*
median (v)	*Median of the components of V*
std (v)	*Standard deviation of the components of V*
sort (v)	*Sorts in ascending order the components of V. For complex it sorts according to the absolute values*

(continued)

sum (v)	*Adds the components of V*
prod (v)	*Multiply the elements of V, with $n! = prod(1:n)$*
cumsum (v)	*Gives the vector of sums accumulated in V*
cumprod (v)	*Gives the vector of products accumulated in V*
diff (v)	*Gives the vector of first differences of V ($V_t - V_{t-1}$)*
gradient (v)	*The gradient of V*
del2 (v)	*Laplacian of V (5-point discrete)*
fft (v)	*Discrete Fourier transform of V*
fft2 (v)	*Two-dimensional discrete Fourier transform of V*
ifft (v)	*Reverse of the discrete Fourier transform of V*
ifft2 (v)	*Inverse of 2-D discrete Fourier transform of V*

These functions also support as an argument a complex matrix, in which case the result is a vector whose components are the results of applying the function to each column of the matrix.

Here are some examples:

```
>> V=2:7, W=[2-i  4i  5+3i]

V =

    2    3    4    5    6    7

W =

   2.0000 - 1.0000i 0 + 4.0000i   5.0000 + 3.0000i

>> diff(V),diff(W)

ans =

    1    1    1    1    1

ans =

   -2.0000 + 5.0000i   5.0000 - 1.0000i

>> cumprod(V),cumsum(V)

ans =

    2         6          24         120        720        5040

ans =

    2    5    9   14   20   27
```

```
>> cumsum(W), mean(W), std(W), sort(W), sum(W)
```

ans =

   2.0000 - 1.0000i   2.0000 + 3.0000i   7.0000 + 6.0000i

ans =

   2.3333 + 2.0000i

ans =

   3.6515

Ans =

   2.0000 + 1.0000i 0 + 4.0000i 5.0000 + 3.0000i

Ans =

   7.0000 + 6.0000i

```
>> mean(V), std(V), sort(V), sum(V)
```

years =

   4.5000

years =

   1.8708

years =

   2   3   4   5   6   7

years =

   27

```
>> fft(W), ifft(W), fft2(W)
```

ans =

   7.0000 + 6.0000i   0.3660 - 0.1699i   -1.3660 - 8.8301i

ans =

   2.3333 + 2.0000i   -0.4553 - 2.9434i   0.1220 - 0.0566i

Ans =

    7.0. 0000i 0.3660 - 0.1699i - 1.3660 - 8.8301i

A.15 Elementary Functions that Support Complex Arrays

- *Trigonometric*

sin (z)	*Sine function*
sinh (z)	*Hyperbolic sine function*
asin (z)	*Arcsine function*
asinh (z)	*Hyperbolic arcsine function*
cos (z)	*Cosine function*
cosh (z)	*Hyperbolic cosine function*
acos (z)	*Arccosine function*
acosh (z)	*Hyperbolic arccosine function*
tan (z)	*Tangent function*
tanh (z)	*Hyperbolic tangent function*
atan (z)	*Arctangent function*
atan2 (z)	*In the fourth quadrant arctangent function*
atanh (z)	*Hyperbolic arctangent function*
sec (z)	*Secant function*
sech (z)	*Hyperbolic secant function*
asec (z)	*Function arccosecant*
asech (z)	*Function arccosecant hyperbolic*
csc (z)	*Function cosecant*
csch (z)	*Function cosecant hyperbolic*
acsc (z)	*Function arccosecant*
acsch (z)	*Hyperbolic arccosecant function*
cot (z)	*Cotangent function*
coth (z)	*Hyperbolic cotangent function*
acot (z)	*Function arccotangent*
acoth (z)	*Arccotangent hyperbolic function*

(*continued*)

- *Exponential*

exp (z)	*Base e exponential function*
log (z)	*Napierian logarithm function*
log10 (z)	*Logarithm base 10 function*
sqrt (z)	*Square root function*

- *Complex*

abs (z)	*Module or absolute value*
angle (z)	*Argument*
conj (z)	*Complex conjugate*
imag (z)	*Imaginary part*
real (z)	*Real part*

- *Numerical*

fix (z)	*Removes the decimals*
floor (z)	*Rounding decimals to the nearest lower integer*
ceil (z)	*Rounds the decimal to the next integer*
round (z)	*Carries out rounding*
rem(z1, z2)	*The remainder of the division of of Z1 by Z2*
sign (z)	*Function sign*

- *Matrix*

simb (z)	*Matrix exponential function by default*
expm1 (z)	*Matrix exponential function in M-file*
expm2 (z)	*Matrix exponential function via Taylor series*
expm3 (z)	*Matrix exponential function via eigenvalues*
logm (z)	*Matrix logarithmic function*
sqrtm (z)	*Matrix square root function*
funm(z,'función')	*It applies the function to the array Z*

Here are some examples:

```
>> A=[7 8 9; 1 2 3; 4 5 6], B=[1+2i 3+i;4+i,i]

A =

    7    8    9
    1    2    3
    4    5    6
```

B =

```
1.0000 + 2.0000i   3.0000 + 1.0000i
4.0000 + 1.0000i        0 + 1.0000i
```

>> without (A), (B), exp (A), exp (B), (B), sqrt (B) log

ans =

```
 0.6570     0.9894     0.4121
 0.8415     0.9093     0.1411
-0.7568    -0.9589    -0.2794
```

ans =

```
 3.1658 + 1.9596i   0.2178 - 1.1634i
-1.1678 - 0.7682i        0 + 1.1752i
```

ans =

```
1. 0e + 003 *

 1.0966     2.9810     8.1031
 0.0027     0.0074     0.0201
 0.0546     0.1484     0.4034
```

ans =

```
 -1.1312 + 2.4717i  10.8523 +16.9014i
 29.4995 +45.9428i   0.5403 + 0.8415i
```

ans =

```
 0.8047 + 1.1071i 1.1513 + 0.3218i
 1.4166 + 0.2450i      0 + 1.5708i
```

ans =

```
 1.2720 + 0.7862i   1.7553 + 0.2848i
 2.0153 + 0.2481i   0.7071 + 0.7071i
```

Exponential functions, square roots and logarithms used above apply element to element to the array and have nothing to do with the exponential matrix and logarithmic functions that are used here.

>> expm(B), logm(A), abs(B), imag(B)

ans =

```
 -27.9191 + 14.8698i -20.0011 +12.0638i
 -24.7950 + 17.6831i -17.5059 + 14.0445i
```

years =

```
  11.9650   12.8038 -  19.9093
 -21.7328  -22.1157    44.6052
  11.8921   12.1200 -  21.2040
```

years =

```
  2.2361 3.1623
  4.1231 1.0000
```

years =

```
  2 1
  1 1
```

>> fix(sin(B)), ceil(log(A)), sign(B), rem(A,3*ones(3))

ans =

```
  3.0000 + 1.0000i       0 - 1.0000i
 -1.0000                 0 + 1.0000i
```

ans =

```
  2     3     3
  0     1     2
  2     2     2
```

ans =

```
  0.4472 + 0.8944i   0.9487 + 0.3162i
  0.9701 + 0.2425i        0 + 1.0000i
```

Ans =

```
  1 2 0
  1 2 0
  1 2 0
```

A.16 Exercises

EXERCISE A-1

Finding the combinations without repetition of 30 elements taken from 12 in 12, the remainder of the division 2^{134} by 3, the decomposition into prime factors of the number 18900, the factorial of 200 and the number N that divided by 16, 24, 30 and 32, gives a remainder of 5.

```
>> factorial (30) / (factorial (12) * factorial(30-12))
```

years =

  8.6493e + 007

Then the command *vpa* is used to present the exact result.

```
>> vpa ' factorial (30) / (factorial (12) * factorial(30-12))' 15
```

years =

86493225.

```
>> rem(2^134,3)
```

years =

    0

```
>> factor (18900)
```

Ans =

    2   2   3   3   3   5   5   7

```
>> factorial (100)
```

Ans =

  9. 3326e + 157

Then use the command *vpa* to present the exact result.

```
>> vpa ' factorial (100)' 160
```

Ans =

9332621544394415268169923885626670049071596826438162146859296389521759999322991560894146397615651828625369792082722375825118521091686400000000000000000000000000.

N-5 is the least common multiple of 16, 24, 30 and 32.

```
>> lcm (lcm (16.24), lcm (30,32))
```

Ans =

  480

Then N = 480 + 5 = 485

EXERCISE A-2

In base 5 the results of the operation defined by $a25aaff6_{16}$ + $6789aba_{12}$ + 35671_8 + 1100221_3 - 1250. Get the result of the operation (666551_7) also in base 13 ($aa199800a_{11}$) + ($fffaaa125_{16}$) / (33331_4 + 6)

The result of the first operation in base 10 is calculated as follows:

>> *base2dec('a25aaf6',16) + base2dec('6789aba',12) +...*
    base2dec('35671',8) + base2dec('1100221',3)-1250

Ans =

   190096544

But still need to pass the previous decimal result base 5.

>> *dec2base (190096544,5)*

Ans =

   342131042134

Then, the final result of the first operation in base 5 is 342131042134.

The result of the second operation in base 10 is calculated as follows:

>> *base2dec('666551',7) * base2dec('aa199800a',11) +...*
    *79 * base2dec('fffaaa125',16) / (base2dec ('33331', 4) + 6)*

Ans =

   2.7537e + 014

We now transform the result into base 13.

>> *dec2base (275373340490852,13)*

Ans =

   BA867963C1496

EXERCISE A-3

In base 13, get the result of the following operation:

(666551_7) ($aa199800a_{11}$) + ($fffaaa125_{16}$) / (33331_4 + 6)

First, we perform the operation in base 10:

A more direct way of doing all of the above is:

```
>> base2dec('666551',7) * base2dec('aa199800a',11) +...
   79 * base2dec('fffaaa125',16) / (base2dec ('33331', 4) + 6)
```

Ans =

   2.753733404908515e + 014

We now transform the result gained 13.

```
>> dec2base (275373340490852,13)
```

Ans =

   BA867963C1496

<hr>

EXERCISE A-4

Given the complex numbers X = 2 + 2i Y = -7 -3$\sqrt{3}$i, calculate Y^3, X^2/Y^{90}, $Y^{1/2}$, $3/2$ and log (X)

```
>> X = 2 + 2 * i; Y =-7-3 * sqrt (3) * i;
>> Y ^ 3
```

years =

   216

```
>> X ^ 2 / Y ^ 90
```

years =

   050180953422426e-085 - 1 + 7.404188256695968e-070i

```
>> sqrt (Y)
```

Ans =

   1.22474487139159-2.12132034355964i

```
>> sqrt(Y^3)
```

Ans =

   14.69693845669907

```
>> log (X)
```

Ans =

   1.03972077083992 + 0.78539816339745i

EXERCISE A-5

Calculate the value of the following operations with complex numbers:

$$\frac{i^8-i^{-8}}{3-4i}+1, \ \ i^{Sin(1+i)}, \ \ \left(2+Ln(i)\right)^{\frac{1}{i}}, \ \ \left(1+i\right)^{i}, \ \ i^{Ln(1+i)}, \ \ \left(1+\sqrt{3}i\right)^{1-i}$$

>> (i ^ 8-i ^(-8)) /(7-4*i) + 1

Ans =

    1

>> i^(sin(1+i))

Ans =

    -0.16665202215166 + 0.329041394503071*i*

>> (2+log(i))^(1/i)

Ans =

    1.15809185259777 1.56388053989023*i*

>> (1+i)^i

Ans =

    0.42882900629437 + 0.15487175246425*i*

>> i^(log(1+i))

Ans =

    0.24911518828716 + 0.15081974484717*i*

>> (1+sqrt(3)*i)^(1-i)

Ans =

    5.34581479196611 + 1.97594883452873*i*

EXERCISE A-6

Calculate real part, imaginary part, mod (abs) and argument of the following:

$$i^{3+i}, \ \left(1+\sqrt{3}i\right)^{1-i}, \ i^{i^i}, \ i^i$$

```
>> Z1 = i^(3+i); Z2 = (1 + sqrt(3) * i)^(1-i); Z3 = (i^i) ^ i; Z4 = i ^ i;

>> format short

>> real ([Z1 Z2 Z3 Z4])
```

ans =

```
    1.0000 5.3458 0.0000 0.2079
```

```
>> imag ([Z1 Z2 Z3 Z4])
```

ans =

```
    0 1.9759 - 1.0000 0
```

```
>> abs ([Z1 Z2 Z3 Z4])
```

ans =

```
    1.0000 5.6993 1.0000 0.2079
```

```
>> angle ([Z1 Z2 Z3 Z4])
```

ans =

```
    0 0.3541 - 1.5708 0
```

EXERCISE A-7

Generate a square matrix of order 4 whose elements are uniform [0,1] random numbers. Generate another square matrix of order 4 whose elements are normal random numbers [0,1]. See generating seeds present, change them to value ½ and rebuild the two arrays of random numbers.

```
>> rand (4)
```

years =

```
    0.9501 0.8913 0.8214 0.9218
    0.2311 0.7621 0.4447 0.7382
    0.6068 0.4565 0.6154 0.1763
    0.4860 0.0185 0.7919 0.4057
```

`>> randn (4)`

years =

```
-0.4326 -1.1465   0.3273 -0.5883
-1.6656   1.1909   0.1746   2.1832
 0.1253   1.1892 -0.1867 -0.1364
 0.2877 -0.0376   0.7258   0.1139
```

`>> rand ('seed')`

Ans =

```
931316785
```

`>> randn ('seed')`

ans =

```
931316785
```

`>> randn ('seed', 1/2)`
`>> rand ('seed', 1/2)`
`>> rand (4)`

years =

```
0.2190 0.9347 0.0346 0.0077
0.0470 0.3835 0.0535 0.3834
0.6789 0.5194 0.5297 0.0668
0.6793 0.8310 0.6711 0.4175
```

`>> randn (4)`

years =

```
1.1650 -0.6965   0.2641   1.2460
0.6268   1.6961   0.8717 -0.6390
0.0751   0.0591 -1.4462   0.5774
0.3516   1.7971 -0.7012 -0.3600
```

EXERCISE A-8

Given the vector variables a = [π,2π,3π,4π,5π] and b = [e, 2e, 3e, 4e, 5e], calculate c = sin (a) + b, d = cos (a), e = Ln (b), f = c * d, g = c/d, h = d ^ 2, i = d ^ 2-e ^ 2 and j = 3d ^ 7-2e ^ 2.

>> a = [pi, 2 * pi, 3 * pi, 4 * pi, 5 * pi], b = [exp (1), 2 * exp (1), 3 * exp (1), 4 * exp (1), 5 * exp (1)], c=sin(a)+b, d=cos(a), e=log(b), f=c.*d, g=c./d, h=d.^2, i=d.^2-e.^2, j=3*d.^7-2*e.^2

a =

   3.1416   6.2832   9.4248   12.5664   15.7080

b =

   2.7183   5.4366   8.1548   10.8731   13.5914

c =

   2.7183   5.4366   8.1548   10.8731   13.5914

d =

   -1   1   -1   1   -1

e =

   1.0000   1.6931   2.0986   2.3863   2.6094

f =

  -2.7183   5.4366   -8.1548   10.8731 -13.5914

g =

  -2.7183   5.4366   -8.1548   10.8731 -13.5914

h =

   1   1   1   1   1

i =

     0   -1.8667   -3.4042   -4.6944   -5.8092

j =

  -5.0000   -2.7335 -11.8083   -8.3888 -16.6183

EXERCISE A-9

Given a uniform random square matrix M of order 3, obtain its inverse and its transposed diagonal. Transform it to a lower triangular matrix and an upper triangular matrix and rotate it 90 degrees. Get the sum of the elements in the first row and the sum of the diagonal elements. Extract the subarray whose diagonal elements are the elements a_{11} and a_{22} and also remove the subarray whose diagonal elements are a_{11} and a_{33}.

>> **M=rand(3)**

M =

```
    0.6868    0.8462    0.6539
    0.5890    0.5269    0.4160
    0.9304    0.0920    0.7012
```

>> **A=inv(M)**

A =

```
   -4.1588    6.6947   -0.0934
    0.3255    1.5930   -1.2487
    5.4758   -9.0924    1.7138
```

>> **B=M'**

B =

```
    0.6868    0.5890    0.9304
    0.8462    0.5269    0.0920
    0.6539    0.4160    0.7012
```

>> **V=diag(M)**

V =

```
    0.6868
    0.5269
    0.7012
```

>> **TI=tril(M)**

TI =

```
    0.6868         0         0
    0.5890    0.5269         0
    0.9304    0.0920    0.7012
```

```
>> TS=triu(M)
```

TS =

0.6868	0.8462	0.6539
0	0.5269	0.4160
0	0	0.7012

```
>> TR=rot90(M)
```

TR =

0.6539	0.4160	0.7012
0.8462	0.5269	0.0920
0.6868	0.5890	0.9304

```
>> s=M(1,1)+M(1,2)+M(1,3)
```

s =

2.1869

```
>> sd=M(1,1)+M(2,2)+M(3,3)
```

sd =

1.9149

```
>> SM=M(1:2,1:2)
```

SM =

0.6868	0.8462
0.5890	0.5269

```
>> SM1=M([1 3], [1 3])
```

SM1 =

0.6868	0.6539
0.9304	0.7012

EXERCISE A-10

Given the complex square matrix M of order 3, get your square, its square root and its exponential base 2 and -2.

$$M = \begin{bmatrix} i & 2i & 3i \\ 4i & 5i & 6i \\ 7i & 8i & 9i \end{bmatrix}$$

```
>> M=[i 2*i 3*i; 4*i 5*i 6*i; 7*i 8*i 9*i]
```

M =

```
   0.0000 + 1.0000i   0.0000 + 2.0000i   0.0000 + 3.0000i
   0.0000 + 4.0000i   0.0000 + 5.0000i   0.0000 + 6.0000i
   0.0000 + 7.0000i   0.0000 + 8.0000i   0.0000 + 9.0000i
```

```
>> C=M^2
```

C =

```
  -30  -36   - 42
  -66  -81   - 96
 -102 -126  - 150
```

```
>> D=M^(1/2)
```

D =

```
   0.8570 - 0.2210i   0.5370 + 0.2445i   0.2169 + 0.7101i
   0.7797 + 0.6607i   0.9011 + 0.8688i   1.0224 + 1.0769i
   0.7024 + 1.5424i   1.2651 + 1.4930i   1.8279 + 1.4437i
```

```
>> 2^M
```

ans =

```
   0.7020 - 0.6146i  -0.1693 - 0.2723i  -0.0407 + 0.0699i
  -0.2320 - 0.3055i   0.7366 - 0.3220i  -0.2947 - 0.3386i
  -0.1661 + 0.0036i  -0.3574 - 0.3717i   0.4513 - 0.7471i
```

```
>> (-2)^M
```

ans =

```
  17.3946 - 16.8443i   4.3404 - 4.5696i  -7.7139 + 7.7050i
   1.5685 -  1.8595i   1.1826 - 0.5045i  -1.2033 + 0.8506i
 -13.2575 + 13.1252i  -3.9751 + 3.5607i   6.3073 - 6.0038i
```

EXERCISE A-11

Given the complex vector $V = [1 + i, i, 1-i]$, find the mean, median, standard deviation, variance, sum, product, maximum and minimum of its elements, as well as its gradient, the discrete Fourier transform and its inverse.

```
>> V = [1 + i, i, 1-i];
 [mean(V),median(V),std(V),var(V),sum(V),prod(V),max(V),min(V)]'
```

ans =

```
 0.6667 - 0.3333i
 1.0000 + 1.0000i
 1.2910
 1.6667
 2.0000 - 1.0000i
      0 - 2.0000i
 1.0000 + 1.0000i
      0 - 1.0000i
```

```
>> gradient(V)
```

ans =

```
 1.0000 - 2.0000i   0.5000 0 + 2.0000i
```

```
>> fft(V)
```

ans =

```
 2.0000 + 1.0000i  -2.7321 + 1.0000i   0.7321 + 1.0000i
```

```
>> ifft(V)
```

ans =

```
 0.6667 + 0.3333i   0.2440 + 0.3333i  -0.9107 + 0.3333i
```

EXERCISE A-12

Given arrays:

$$A = \begin{bmatrix} 1 & 1 & 0 \\ 0 & 1 & 1 \\ 0 & 0 & 1 \end{bmatrix} \quad B = \begin{bmatrix} i & 1-i & 2+i \\ 0 & -1 & 3-i \\ 0 & 0 & -i \end{bmatrix} \quad C = \begin{bmatrix} 1 & 1 & 1 \\ 0 & sqrt(2)i & -sqrt(2)i \\ 1 & -1 & -1 \end{bmatrix}$$

Calculate $AB - B$, $A^2 + B^2 + C^2$, ABC, sqrt (A) + sqrt (B) + sqrt(C), $(e^A + e^B + e^C)$, their transposes and their inverses. Also check that any matrix is multiplied by its inverse obtains the identity matrix.

```
>> A=[1 1 0;0 1 1;0 0 1]; B=[i 1-i 2+i;0 -1 7-i;0 0 -i]; C=[1 1 1; 0 sqrt(2)*i
-sqrt(2)*i;1 -1 -1];
```

```
>> M1=A*B-B*A
```

M1 =

```
   0        -1.0000 - 1.0000i   2.0000
   0               0            1.0000 - 1.0000i
   0               0                   0
```

```
>> M2=A^2+B^2+C^2
```

M2 =

```
   2.0000          2.0000 + 3.4142i   3.0000 - 5.4142i
        0 - 1.4142i  -0.0000 + 1.4142i   0.0000 - 0.5858i
        0            2.0000 - 1.4142i   2.0000 + 1.4142i
```

```
>> M3=A*B*C
```

M3 =

```
   5.0000 + 1.0000i   -3.5858 + 1.0000i   -6.4142 + 1.0000i
   3.0000 - 2.0000i   -3.0000 + 0.5858i   -3.0000 + 3.4142i
        0 - 1.0000i         0 + 1.0000i         0 + 1.0000i
```

```
>> M4=sqrtm(A)+sqrtm(B)-sqrtm(C)
```

M4 =

```
   0.6356 + 0.8361i   -0.3250 - 0.8204i   3.0734 + 1.2896i
   0.1582 - 0.1521i    0.0896 + 0.5702i   3.3029 - 1.8025i
  -0.3740 - 0.2654i    0.7472 + 0.3370i   1.2255 + 0.1048i
```

```
>> M5=expm(A)*(expm(B)+expm(C))

M5 =

  14.1906 - 0.0822i    5.4400 + 4.2724i   17.9169 - 9.5842i
   4.5854 - 1.4972i    0.6830 + 2.1575i    8.5597 - 7.6573i
   3.5528 + 0.3560i    0.1008 - 0.7488i    3.2433 - 1.8406i

>> inv(A)

years =

    1 -1  1
    0 -1 -1
    0  0  1

>> inv(B)

ans =

    0 - 1.0000i  -1.0000 - 1.0000i  -4.0000 + 3.0000i
    0               -1.0000           1.0000 + 3.0000i
    0                0                    0 + 1.0000i

>> inv(C)

ans =

  0.5000            0            0.5000
  0.2500        0 - 0.3536i     -0.2500
  0.2500        0 + 0.3536i     -0.2500

>> [A*inv(A) B*inv(B) C*inv(C)]

years =

    1    0    0    1    0    0    1    0    0
    0    1    0    0    1    0    0    1    0
    0    0    1    0    0    1    0    0    1

>> A'

years =

    1 0 0
    1 1 0
    0 1 1
```

>> B'

years =

0 - 1.0000i	0	0
1.0000 + 1.0000i	-1.0000	0
2.0000 - 1.0000i	3.0000 + 1.0000i	0 + 1.0000i

>> C'

ans =

1.0000	0	1.0000
1.0000	0 - 1.4142i	-1.0000
1.0000	0 + 1.4142i	-1.0000

Get the eBook for only $10!

Now you can take the weightless companion with you anywhere, anytime. Your purchase of this book entitles you to 3 electronic versions for only $10.

This Apress title will prove so indispensible that you'll want to carry it with you everywhere, which is why we are offering the eBook in 3 formats for only $10 if you have already purchased the print book.

Convenient and fully searchable, the PDF version enables you to easily find and copy code—or perform examples by quickly toggling between instructions and applications. The MOBI format is ideal for your Kindle, while the ePUB can be utilized on a variety of mobile devices.

Go to www.apress.com/promo/tendollars to purchase your companion eBook.

CPSIA information can be obtained
at www.ICGtesting.com
Printed in the USA
LVHW10s1501190918
590616LV00010B/71/P